# Perfect Power in Consciousness

## Seeking Truth Through the Subconscious and Superconscious Mind

### Dr. Heather Anne Harder

## ISBN 1-884410-01-4

Published by

LIGHT PUBLISHING

210 S. Main Street, Suite 203
Crown Point, IN 46307
(219) 662-7248

a division of

The Association of Universal Light Volunteers
210 S. Main Street, Suite 202
Crown Point, IN 46307
(219) 662-7074

Printed in the United States of America

# ACKNOWLEDGMENTS

This is a very special time on Earth. Most people are becoming ever aware of a sense of urgency, even if they are unaware of the details. There is no longer time to linger on projects at hand. When the need to take action is felt, then action must be taken quickly. This book is such a project. Spirit guidance dictated the need of this book to be released. Something big is about to happen/shift and this book will assist people to move through this shift with more comfort. Please share this book with others so many can read it as quickly as possible.

This book is meant to be read with the heart and not the mind. The mind will find flaws and argue the content. Read for the personal message it offers and the truth it contains. As with all books you read, I suggest you begin by saying a prayer and asking for guidance and discernment. This will allow you to recognize and accept your own truth. After all, it is time to learn to trust your own inner guidance.

When spirit gives a task and you work at your maximum capacity, much help is provided. So it was with this project. My Earthly helpers have been miracle workers. Kay Olrich's insights gave rise to the perfect title. Margaret Pinyon was a wonderful support during the editing process. Linda Kuester provided invaluable aid in typing the material. Brian Kuss, Light Publishing Coordinator, has been an incredible asset to the publishing process. Kerri Anne Harder, Adrianne Bacavis and Anna Rominger have offered suggestions and assistance with the flow of the message. Doris Bishop, my dear third-dimensional friend, poured tirelessly over the manuscript editing, correcting and refining. Her detailed-oriented mind was ever willing to provide service to the cause. She also offered great moral support as she transformed into a fourth-dimensional person while working on this book, complete with physical cleansing and awareness shifts. These people provided the physical services needed to complete this project.

I also want to thank my family, who provided for themselves when necessary and allowed me the time to do God's work. Bob, Kerri and Stacie are heaven's gifts to me. They keep me anchored into reality and bathed in love.

I wish to thank my many friends and students who have provided much encouragement, support and incentive to write *Perfect Power in Consciousness*. Appreciation goes to Heather Slamon and Hope Burton for helping me keep my life in order and Mark Roser, who will never know the service he provides me with his confidence in me and my work. When I need a boost, he is always there.

Finally, I wish to acknowledge the miraculous service given by my friends from other dimensions. They alter time, people and events to make all things possible. If you wish to contact them, go within, for they are waiting eagerly for you. Over the years, their messages have provided insight, unconditional love and guidance. They have kept me going when the physical me was willing to quit. I repeat my pledge to offer to others a little of what they have given to me. Some of their messages are included in this book so that you too may benefit from their wisdom.

Finally, my deepest gratitude goes to the Divine Infinite Intelligence, known by many names throughout the universe, for sharing so much with me and allowing me to share with others.

# Table of Contents

## *Recognizing Your Potential for Greatness*

We are living in an exciting and often confusing time. Humanity wishes to slow the pace and make sense of the process. But indeed, that is not possible. Even if it were possible, you would not really choose to do so. For in that action would come a violation of all that you came to achieve. This is the time of acceleration, a time of awakening. All feel the excitement and all know in the innermost recesses of their beingness that now is the time. Instantly, the question arises: Yes, it is time; but time for what?

Well, dear folks, this book is designed to tell you about the day that is upon you. It will give you a glimpse at the day that is to come. For, indeed, today will influence tomorrow. If you live the now in Divine harmony, then your tomorrows will be enhanced. Humanity has lived in the past and the present, but has been afraid to open to the now. Now requires you to be responsible, and that has not always been desired. It is easier to play the victim and cast blame on others.

Now is the time to shed the three-dimensional reality that has bound you to the limits of physical existence and spread your wings to fly as the children of God were designed to do. Just as the young sparrow must take lessons from the experienced bird, so too must you follow in the path of others who have achieved before you. They do not dictate the way, for each of you must discover that yourself. Instead, those who have come before encourage you and challenge you to try your wings and leave the comfort of the familiar. Just as the young bird has all flight potential latent in its being, so, too, does humanity. Like the bird, you must jump out of the safe and comfortable, and risk, in order to achieve the greatness of your destiny.

## *Brain, Mind and Reality*

n your head lies a wondrous three-pound miracle. This dull, pinkish-gray gelatinous glob is about the size of two human fists. To look at it, one would never be aware of its constant action or its fantastic capabilities. The brain's basic functions are known, but many aspects are still beyond the comprehension of scientists. Some scientists think they have found the answers. They write book after book to tell you all they know about the brain. The trouble is, if you read several books, they are contradictory. Each author wants to convince you he/she is right and everyone else is wrong. If you are to understand and recognize reality, you must begin with some basic concept of the brain and its role in the development of your reality.

The brain/mind relationship is a marvelous swirl of matter and energy; they are inseparable in their ongoing purpose of existence. The brain is where the mind contemplates itself. It reflects on its own achievement, tasks and needs. In the celebrated case of Sybil, whose brain possessed the ability to project seventeen distinct personalities, each personality chose a different perspective from which to view the world (Restak, 1984). Each had values, behaviors and an expression of ideas that were unique to each personality. Some personalities had talents that the others lacked. Obviously, each of the Sybil fragments could have done everything, but the fragmented mind did not know and/or believe it and therefore couldn't. Each aspect of Sybil had its own reality.

Twenty years ago researchers said that a person used only ten percent of the brain. Now many researchers agree that the amount utilized is less than one percent (Russell, 1979). If you could double that to just two percent, think of the knowledge you would give the world. No government funding is needed. Only one brain, perhaps yours, is needed to open the door for all brains to follow. It is time you give your brain the knowledge that it is confined only by its own self-imposed limits. The time is upon you to transcend these limits of physicality and be all that you can be. But to do this you must first believe it. To believe it you must have proof. Therefore, you shall learn more about the brain. Sources have been cited so you can read more about this wondrous glob if you wish to explore further. The more you learn, the more impressed you will be.

A much closer look at the brain reveals individual cells. They look like a drop of paint blown in all directions by using a straw. The drop of paint is analogous to the cell body that contains the nucleus; the arms are the dendrites. The cell body also has a special filament known as an axon. The dendrites never touch one another; therefore, they must pick up signals from each other in a "spark-gap" fashion, called a *synapse*. The message is taken to the cell body, then passes through the axon at speeds up to 225 miles per hour to its destination within the brain.

This is, of course, a simplistic, two-dimensional description of a complicated, three-dimensional process. There are thirty billion cell bodies in the brain and each can have as many as sixty thousand dendrites, not to mention 150 to 300 billion glial cells. Glial cells feed the cell bodies and maintain space between neurons. As many as one hundred fifty thousand signals can be processed in the brain, simultaneously exerting control over all that the body does, says and feels (Ratcliff, 1975). The brain is capable of recording 1,000 bits of information per second, from the day of birth through old age and will still have storage capacity to spare (Russell, 1979). Only now do you begin to get a picture of the brain's complexity.

An incident brought home to me the brain's incredible capabilities. When my niece was seven months old, she was accidentally shot in the head with a pellet gun at point-blank range. After a fight for her life, she survived with the bullet still lodged in her brain. From a frontal x-ray the bullet is located between her eyes; from a side view it is one inch above and one inch behind her ear. Doctors would not remove the bullet for fear of the further damage surgery would cause. Since the bullet is lodged in the motor section of the brain, one would expect to see some impairment in these abilities. Perhaps damage would also be caused along the bullet's entering pathway. Yet, at age fourteen, she has absolutely no impairment in any area. During a CAT scan, it was learned that the brain had totally encased the bullet in scar tissue. Any fear of the bullet moving and causing further damage has been eliminated.

According to Dr. Marvin Languis, author of *Brain and Learning: Directions in Early Childhood Education*, the bullet probably changed her; but the brain has the unlimited capacity to reorganize its own information and repair any damage to itself. Even after the bullet passed through her brain and rested in the motor area, the brain was able to rebuild and reroute all the information so that no motor skills or abilities were lost.

If my niece was able to make the most of her brain and overcome this major obstacle, then I, too, wanted to make the most of my mental capabilities. I wanted to use more than the one percent that everyone else was using. So began my quest for brain/mind power. . .

# The Secret of Mind Power

Thus, I started digging into mind research. I started by looking at brain-wave patterns. When the first research was conducted on brain waves, subjects were asked to lie down and be hooked up to machines that recorded images of the mind at work. The brain-wave patterns displayed were called *alpha* waves. Researchers thought this was the pattern of the mind. But they soon discovered that when people got up and moved around, their brain waves changed. These new patterns were called *beta* waves.

When you are up and going about the process of life, you are usually functioning in beta wave patterns. When you think hard, your brain displays beta waves, which indicates the mind is in motion. Beta level, however, is not where you mind works best. If you are lying around daydreaming, you generate alpha waves. It is believed that the alpha waves hold the secret of the unlimited ability of the mind.

As the studies continued, two additional patterns were found. *Theta* waves are even slower than alpha waves. These occur during that drifting-off-to-sleep time. *Delta* waves occur during the period when you are in "la-la land."

There are many stories of geniuses who were frequent daydreamers. Many, like Einstein and Edison, did not do well in school because of it. They, on the other hand, felt they received insights and solutions to their problems when they were daydreaming. The story is told of Einstein formulating his theory of relativity while sitting under a tree. Einstein valued his daydreaming, for he claimed, "Imagination is everything." During a conference on "Education and the Future" held in the 1960s, a team including representatives from the National Aeronautics and Space Administration (NASA) stated that members of the space team were being trained to daydream from twenty minutes to two hours each day because it is in this state that highly creative solutions emerge.

It is the alpha wave state that seems to offer the greatest access to one's mental capacities while in a conscious state. It appears that when you let go of the focusing process, you do your more productive mental work. It is the alpha state that is reached during meditation. If you are always working hard or pushing yourself, you may not be using your mind efficiently. It is important to remember that you have four different mental levels or states, and you need to include all of them in your life.

Understanding how the mind functions is the first step toward better utilization of its capabilities. It has been said, *Whatever the mind can conceive and believe, it can achieve* (Hill, 1960). If you vividly imagine something, you create the same brain pattern as when actually performing the task. Being in a relaxed, alpha state increases your chance for success.

To illustrate this I would like you to relax your body and share the following story. Allow your mind to create the reality of the experience. Are you ready? Now imagine, really imagine the following scene:

> **Exercise:** You are at home and you are feeling hungry. You walk into the kitchen and look around. You see nothing that appeals to you. So you walk over to the refrigerator and open the door. Your eyes fall on a large lemon. You decide to have it. You take it out and cut it into quarters. You place one quarter in your mouth and bite down. You feel the tart juice fill your mouth.

Did you have a reaction? Did your mouth water? Could you taste the lemon? This story illustrates how words impact you and create your reality. It illustrates how that reality impacts your physical existence. Because your mind created the reality of this experience, you had a physical reaction to an imaginary experience.

Under hypnosis, when people were told that they were going to be touched with a burning hot poker, they produced all the physical reactions of pain up to and including a blister where the skin was touched. Yet they had been touched with only a pencil point. Because the mind believed, it created its own reality.

Indian yogi Swami Roma visited the Menninger Foundation at Topeka, Kansas, in 1970. He displayed his extraordinary abilities to control his own bodily functions. He could alter the temperature of two patches of skin a few inches apart by as much as ten degrees. He could make one hot and the other cold by visualizing ice on one area and a hot coal on the other. His body responded as if it were fact. He was also able to stop his heart from pumping blood, not through the normal way of slowing the heart rate, but by increasing his heartbeats to 300 beats per minute without blood passing through its chambers. Not only could he do these things, as well as perform other feats, but he was also able to control his own brain waves (Buzan, 1984).

These early experiences gave rise to biofeedback research and training. Now those who want to learn this art can program their own brain/mind to respond. Biofeedback has proven to have a positive effect on physical health, athletic performance, mental ability, motivation and will-power (Restak, 1979). It is done by first learning it is possible. Until people believe they can control these things, they are unable to do so. Experimental and clinical psychologists have proven beyond a doubt that the brain is unable to differentiate between actual experiences and experiences imagined vividly in detail

(Maltz, 1960). Our brain/minds must be taught to visualize success, peace, accomplishments and other positive qualities. Unfortunately, they are often fed a diet of "You can't," "You won't," "Don't be stupid," or other such mind-binders.

The apparent limits of the human brain and mind are only the limits of what you believe is possible and/or impossible (Russell, 1979).

The brain/mind combination is truly miraculous, but even more miraculous is the brain's ability to automatically control itself and the body. It constantly monitors its own temperature, water level and oxygen level. For example, if your carbon dioxide level is rising in your blood and more oxygen is needed, the brain will step up the breathing rate by accelerating the contraction and relaxation of chest muscles. One indication of the brain's importance is the amount of resources allocated to the brain. Although the brain represents only two percent of body weight, it requires twenty percent of the oxygen and a fifth of the blood supply (Ratcliff, 1975).

All this power--yet no one seems to know or care what potential lies just beyond our awareness. More people know how their car works than understand even the basic workings of their brain. People generally take better care of their car than they do the mental processes of their brain. No one would ever dream of getting in an automobile, stepping on the gas and not steering. Yet for many, their lives are the automobile and the brain is the steering mechanism that is never consciously touched. They let fate do the driving. Thank goodness the brain has an automatic pilot. If taking control of all aspects of your life and mental awareness is not important to you, or if you think you are unable to control the process, then your auto pilot will do those things for you. As you move into fourth and fifth dimensions, you will no longer be satisfied with auto pilot. You will want to take over the wheel and assume responsibility and control of your life. Are you ready?

It has been scientifically proven that you do have control over those areas you previously believed uncontrollable. Until you are ready to take control of those functions on a conscious level, your pulse, heartbeat, body temperature, breathing rate and other important functions are taken care of automatically. The more you are aware of the potential of the brain/mind, the more in control you can be. You may never want to take over many of these bodily functions. But if you are on a camping trip far from a town and you fall and break your leg, you may choose to reduce your brain's perception of pain. If you cut yourself and are bleeding badly, you could reduce and even stop the bleeding by using the brain/mind power. You could heal a blister if burned, or lower your breathing rate if enclosed in an area where oxygen is scarce. You wouldn't want to assume conscious control over all body functions, but the ability to do so has practical applications in emergency situations. Your brain/mind has the power to heal every hurt that the physical body experiences. Knowing you have this capacity also allows you to open your door of awareness to other even greater capacities. Even if you don't really believe you have total control over every aspect of your life, start pretending that every word and every thought will become your reality. Then watch the changes in your life.

I have shared some pretty impressive thoughts concerning your mind. The problem is that sometimes this all-powerful, all-knowing mind can actually hold you back from our being all you can be. It has been too empowered for too long. The mind has simply gotten too big for its own good. I know that this can come as a shock for some of you so let me take a moment to explain.

*Mental clarity, as you have known it, is a thing of the past. In order to make your spiritual ascension, you must lose your mind!* Wow! I lost some of you on that one, I'm sure. So let me explain what mental clarity is and why it is something that must give way for truth and beauty to prevail.

Now that you have settled down a little, let me explain. You won't literally lose your mind, but you do have to let go of much of the automatic and control *power* of the mind. Now, does that make you feel better? The all-powerful mind which we have honored and encouraged is actually the last obstacle which humanity must overcome in order to take its rightful place in the spiritual hierarchy. Now for the reasons.

## THE MIND LIMITS----------

Your mind is the governing device that scales down All-That-Is into comprehensible bite-size pieces. Because of your creative nature in this third-dimensional-linear-and-logical world you had to have some way to diminish your totality into a physically limited existence. This is the function of the mind.

Research has proven that you take in zillions times more data than you realize. For instance, at a large party you may be consciously aware of the conversation you are having with two friends, while unaware of all the other conversations going on in the room. Yet careful research has shown that under hypnosis, you not only are aware of them but can repeat them all verbatim. (This same unlimited ability of perception and retention is documented for all your physical senses.)

It is the mind, at least the conscious part, that limits your awareness. In short, you take in unlimited bits of information while the mind determines, actually lessens, your awareness to what it thinks you can handle and plunks all the rest of the data safely away into your subconscious.

Your conscious mind alone determines what you attend to and then blocks out the rest. If you were to smell smoke while conversing, your mind would change your focus and alert you to a possible danger. This would cause you to be distracted from your friends. If, while talking, you were to hear someone mention your name, your mind would again alert you to the possible conversation about you, and you would tune into that conversation. None of these are things *you* choose. It is *your mind that chooses for you*. It is the mind that determines through *its own will* what you may focus on and then maintains close watch to see that your awareness does not wander into other areas, which your mind alone has deemed off limits to you.

This is much like a prisoner who has very clear boundaries or limits set for him/her by the guards. Your mind is your guard and as long as it is in total control; you are its prisoner. Humanity has not rebelled over this control rather it has applauded the mind for its ability to focus and even encouraged its narrow range of operation by developing whole thinking curriculums for children starting as young as kindergarten! If only we could learn to unleash humanity's full potential rather than applaud the mind's limitations.

The mind's system of limitation has worked well over eons of time and has even served humanity. After all, if you were aware of all the data that you take into your brain each second, you would be overwhelmed and might possibly go mad. You needed the mind to limit. Thus, it served the totality of you to give the mind the power to limit and control your totality. Notice that the mind is separate from you. *You* are the soul/spirit creation of the God Essence. This you, what I lovingly refer to as the big You (notice the capital "Y"), is unlimited. The big You has a mind, but You are not your mind. The you that is controlled and limited by the mind is what I call the little you (notice the lower case "y"). The little you has also been called the personality/ego and is totally influenced by the mind. The big You is unlimited, and is influenced by the Divine Source. The big You is spontaneous and follows its intuition and internal guidance even when this guidance is not logical and thus does not make sense.

Unfortunately, it is the mind that decides what makes sense and what does not. If the mind agrees with the information, then it gives its approval. If the mind disagrees with the information, then it generates lots of evidence to convince *you* that it isn't right, doesn't make sense, and that it isn't logical. All this is part of the process to keep you controlled and limited. The mind's whole purpose is to limit. Now, don't start picking on the mind. It means well.

The mind, which has a consciousness of its own, was given the duty to guard what you were to be able to focus and attend. This was quite heady for the mind, and the mind took it very seriously. Thus the mind has become a tyrant. Now we are in the position of needing to break through this mental stronghold to again claim our unlimited possibilities.

Just like a mother who cautions her child to stay in the yard to avoid possible harm, so, too, does the mind want to keep you safe. This is an important job and over the years you have needed it because you wouldn't let the real You come through and be responsible. Now the times are changing and it is the You who must again gain control and free yourself from the shackles of the mind. This will again allow YOU your unlimited potential.

It is time once again to be aware of All-That-Is in a simultaneous fashion; not in a logical and linear fashion but in a holistic manner. For many people it is like living in an eight-track world. You become aware of the many subtleties and strata of life all happening at once. At first, it is very distracting and you may have difficulty focusing on a single thing but gradually, as trust and comfort with the new perceptions grow, the need to maintain focus dies away. You begin to live in the experience and not be concerned with maintaining a limited focus. This is the first of many changes in the expansion of powers.

## *THE MIND DISTRACTS----------*

The mind does not wish to give up its place of power so it struggles with you over dominance. When you sit quietly, it is the mind that reminds you of all the things you *should* be doing. It knows that sitting quietly is one of the ways you break through its barriers. During meditation, it can cause you to lose consciousness, as if you were asleep, for it fears letting you reach for the stars which are easily yours in this meditative state. So it merely shuts down and refuses to let you play.

One way to test to see if it is truly sleep or the mind's open show of dominance is to put on a guided meditation. If you go to sleep but wake up at the end of the meditation, you weren't truly asleep; rather your mind was blocking the experience. Don't worry about it; you are still getting the experience. The mind can only block the *awareness* of the experience; it cannot block the experience. Thus the mind cannot block the growth. So continue to do the meditation or visualization, and eventually the stronghold of the mind will be broken and a new harmonious relationship will emerge.

If your mind is creating a distraction, then you must lovingly and firmly let your mind know that that is no longer allowed or desired. Treat it like a rebellious toddler. You can dominate it with sheer force but that only creates inner disharmony, and you really aren't much better off. Instead talk to your mind and reassure it that you are a big girl/boy and that You, the soul/spirit part of you, are ready to take control of your life and that it must also learn to work in harmony with the totality of you. Thank it for all that it has done for you and be genuine with your appreciation, for truly the mind has allowed you to come this far. It is just time to now move beyond all limits, and you must have the mind's cooperation for that. Otherwise you will be besieged with all the reasons why you must continue to live a life of limits and discontinue your growth. The mind is a powerful generator of reasons why things won't work! It is best to get it to work with you in peace, love and harmony.

## THE MIND CREATES----------

You may be aware of our ability to create, and thoughts *do* create. Each thought the mind entertains is a creative thought-form, or unit of energy. This unit of energy has no beginning, nor ending, but is an individuation of the totality of energy. When enough mental energy has centered on a single thought, that thought takes physical form or manifests.

Unfortunately, the mind often ponders all the lesser elements of life. It thinks about destruction, hate, greed, violence and in doing so actually empowers these lesser elements. Thus the mind creates what it does not desire because it doesn't know any better. The mind does not realize that it does not work in negatives but instantly transforms them into positives which are then created. That may sound confusing, but let me give you a simple example.

If I tell you, "Don't think of monkeys," what is your first thought? Monkeys, of course. See, even though you did not want to think of monkeys, and you may have even given yourself that command, your mind instantly jumped to monkeys. It has no choice because the mind cannot accept a negative statement like *don't*; it automatically converts it to a positive and then creates it.

The mind also judges, evaluates and analyzes, and in doing so, creates these thoughts, too. If you judge another to be greedy, your mind then creates many situations for greed to form in your life as you begin to measure everyone to this imaginary yardstick called greed. Thus the mind helps to bring into creation that which it may want to avoid.

The creative abilities were originally part of the soul/spirit not the mind. The mind did not, and does not, have the purity to manifest but has taken on the ability anyway. Once the mind is silenced then this Divine creative ability can again come from the Source. The soul/spirit only knows the joy and beauty of its source. Artists, who are in touch with the Infinite Intelligence will tell you that they never think about what they are creating; they only allow it to take form through them.

Luckily, the mind thinks in many directions so that your thoughts often cancel themselves out by the mental conflict. This has been a salvation for humanity who would have long destroyed itself without this conflict. Humanity's propensity for negative thinking created a greater need for the mind to chatter. This chatter caused a distraction and a lessening of the ability to create with a single thought. You may have accepted this chatter to be normal. If you have ever attended a little league baseball game, you have seen this system in action. A young batter steps to the mound, and all the players from the opposing team start yelling "Hey batter, hey batter" along with lots of other words. This chatter is designed to break the batter's concentration so they won't hit the ball. For the most part it works.

Our mental chatter was designed to break our concentration so that every thought did not instantly manifest into our lives. Because of your distorted and unhealthy thoughts, it is lucky for you that it works. I equate this chatter to carrying around a back-seat driver. If you have ever gone to a show and had somebody sitting near you who insisted on talking throughout the movie, you know how distracting it can be. Usually you do whatever is necessary to encourage them to listen to the movie; but if they insist on talking, it is quite possible that you may tune them out and become oblivious to their chatter. So it is with the mind. You have become so used to the chatter that you don't even realize that it is a distraction because it has become the norm.

## THE MIND HOLDS ON----------

People brag about having a mind like a steel trap. What they mean, and take pride in, is the fact that their mind won't let go. We call it memory and humanity values it. Memory does have a purpose, but it too has gotten out of hand. We now hold on to old trivia, (Who really cares what Mr. Ed's first words were?) and most unfortunately we hold on to old beliefs. Because we once were sure of the nature of reality, we hang on to that belief for dear life, even when it no longer fits with our new reality.

## CHANGING REALITIES
## REQUIRES CHANGING THE MIND----------

Humanity is now in the process of moving from a third-dimensional reality to a greater reality. Those old mental patterns no longer serve, so they must be broken down and the mind restored to its rightful place. This means it must work harmoniously with the body and the soul/spirit. Now the limits and the limiting nature of the mind must be broken up and expanded. Sounds good...except you have become very familiar with the ways of the old. The limits were comforting and the ways of the new are often confusing.

As our mind is expanded, you become aware of all that is around you. It can be confusing and distracting. You wonder why your mind wanders. You no longer maintain that comfortable, but limiting, focus. You may think you are losing your mind, but in reality you are gaining and attaining your unlimited nature. It can be compared to lying on the ground watching a blade of grass, then being raised above the grass a hundred or perhaps a thousand feet and pondering the same blade of grass. At this height it is much more difficult to even see it, let alone ponder it. Your vision takes in so much that you are distracted by the totality and the wonder of the scene.

When you long for the clarity of the small mental scene, take a deep breath and recognize the beauty of the larger picture. It is not old age, senility nor even Alzheimer's disease that makes you become lost in your sea of images and experiences. It is the expansiveness of your new realities that allow you to play in those new realities. Your blinders are being removed so you can experience it all. At first it can be distracting but over time it will become familiar.

All thought forms must be literally broken up and discarded in order to make room for new ones. This causes a haziness of thoughts almost like a mental fog. Nothing seems to fit and you can't seem to hold onto a reality. You can't quite hold onto or reach a mental thought although you may know one exists.

You exist in a mist of unformed essence just beyond your grasp. It can be both scary and frustrating. Working, especially thinking, can be extremely challenging. You feel like you are losing your mind and indeed you are...the old, outdated, but familiar, version of your mind.

I have often equated this to walking through a waterfall. As you first approach the waterfall, you might experience a pleasant, light mist but as you get closer the mist becomes overwhelming. You can't seem to grasp a thought and everything is distracting. As you walk through it, you will again experience the mist and finally a new reality. When you are on the other side, it will seem strange that walking through the waterfall was ever a concern.

These periods can last from a few days to a few weeks, but they do give way to a greater and more beautiful reality. When these periods would descend upon me, I learned to just enjoy them and consider them a mental vacation of sorts. . .a time to experience life in a new way. I played and did the best I could with whatever I had to do. I asked the angels to assist me as I moved from the known into the unknown.

There are many products which profess to bring you mental clarity, but all the blue-green algae in the world will not eliminate this process because you must move through it in order to get beyond the limits of the mind. It is a joyful state of growth but, much like entering school for the first time, it can be scary. Trust the process and experience the joy and let your inner guidance lead the way.

## THE MIND DETERMINES
## YOUR DIMENSIONAL REALITY----------

Understanding the brain/mind's role in creating your reality brings you back to the realization that your "reality" is what your brain/mind *perceives* as reality. Now, back to your perceptions of reality.

Listen to your mind reaffirm your personal reality as the discussion of reality unfolds here. If you hear yourself thinking, "That's what it is...there is no doubt about it!" take note that this is an indication of your dimensional reality. Your friends may perceive other truths or have another dimensional reality. Both are correct; therefore, do not attempt to convince another to accept your truth. Recognize that you each have different perceptions of reality. Each of you is correct, because your *mind* creates your reality! The reality you accept on a daily basis is a reflection of the dimension in which you exist. *The dimension is a state of consciousness.* Your consciousness is a reflection of your mind's accepted truth. You must learn to respect each person's reality. Only through respect can you open yourself to new awareness and new worlds.

Your truth, or at least what the mind accepts as your truth, determines your dimension of existence and vice versa. Dimension is not a destination or a place to go, like a trip to another state or a movie theater. Your dimensional state is a state of consciousness, an orientation to your world. It is how you view life. Your orientation to "reality" is determined by your dimension of consciousness. It is a mental and vibrational state of being. The dimension in which you exist determines what is real in your life.

I intend to describe the various dimensions, but telling you about each dimension is much like telling a Martian about life on Earth. As everyone knows, there is an unlimited number of experiences one can have while experiencing life. Looking at a much smaller issue, if I had ten people describe toast, each would do it in a different way using different words and analogies. Each might describe toast through their own perceptions of taste, texture, feel, sound, smell or appearance. Each person would describe toast through his/her personal experiences in his/her own words and concepts, stressing what is perceived to be the most important qualities of toast. As I attempt to describe the dimensions of consciousness, I must use words and concepts that come from a third-dimensional vocabulary. I must use analogies that have reality in my life. Others describing the same aspect from the same dimension may describe that aspect differently. There are a multitude of aspects of experiences within each dimension. Therefore, be aware that the following is my truth about the various dimensional consciousnesses, as filtered through my vocabulary, experiences and mental consciousness.

## *Climbing the Tree of Life*

 tree is best used to illustrate the levels of dimensional consciousness. In the beginning is the seed--the promise and potential of all things to come. As the tree grows it must first put roots in the ground, for without them the tree cannot exist. This process of grounding is important. The deeper and stronger the roots, the higher it can grow and the more sway it can tolerate. Over time, the tree seedling emerges from the ground. It grows in stature and complexity, producing wondrous branches in all directions.

If you can imagine yourself as a bird sitting on that tree during its growth, you would first experience reality from the point of view of the sprout and the roots seeking nourishment and a supportive environment. At first you would view the world from the ground level, seeing only the blades of grass, the feet of larger animals, the ants and only the stems and shoots of the taller plants. As the tree grows taller, you would see beyond the grass level and look down upon the flowers and perhaps not see their stems. The patterns of beauty would become apparent as you viewed the scene from a higher perspective. Increasingly you would recognize flower beds and landscaping patterns, but you would loose the ability to see the uniqueness of each blade of grass. You must give up one vision to see another. Still your vision changes as the tree grows. As branches develop and extend themselves, they each afford you a different view.

From the very top of the highest tree you see the patterns, the interrelationships of the different plants and animals. The sky blends with the ground, the water nourishes and the wind impacts. From the highest point on the highest tree, reality seems very different than when perceived at the root level. One view is not better than another;

it is simply different. One is more complete and inclusive, but not superior to the other. Both are correct--and real.

So it is with your perception of reality. It reflects your dimensional truth; it does not denote your superiority. It is inappropriate to force another to look at reality from your branch against that person's will. It is also inappropriate to force your dimensional thought patterns on someone else. It is perfectly acceptable to tell another about your view and offer to lend a hand to anyone wanting to climb the tree. You offer and the other person may accept or decline the offer. It is that person's right to choose (free will). Nor is that person better than or less competent than you because of that choice.

If you complete your climb to the top of the tree, it does not mean that you would always view the world from there. You may want to lower yourself and move among the branches or even climb down to look again from the root's vantage point. You would have the choice and could move freely. And so it is with dimensional reality. Just because you function comfortably at one level does not mean that at times you may not move into another for exploration or review. This too is perfectly normal.

Know that the various levels of dimensional consciousness reflect your truth. That is not what you think, but what you know. Because it is your truth, no one can make you believe otherwise. It is also important to accept and respect all truths and those who embrace them. Just as you would not force your truth on another, you should not feel you must accept someone else's truth as your own. Even if the person is bigger, smarter, has more degrees, is older or wiser, it is still vitally important that you sift the information given (their truth) through your own heart filter and see how you feel about it. Trust your ability to discriminate between truth and illusion. Your truth is *your* truth. If you accept everything told to you as your truth, you will go nuts...and that's the truth!

You might ask, "What comes first, the truth or the belief in the truth?" It is impossible to answer. For some people, affirming the truth they wish to experience brings about the reality that makes it true. For example, if I affirm, "God provides me with a life filled with love and abundance," over and over again, I may start to believe it. I will begin to see examples of love and abundance in my life. As I grow to expect love and abundance, I pull these things to my awareness and they become more prevalent in my life. I no longer have to affirm this statement as truth because it has become my reality. Other people may not affirm this statement, but over time they may recognize the blessings in their life because they are open to them and come to the same truth through life experiences. In truth, it does not matter.

## *Third-Dimensional Consciousness*

Your most basic--and initial--perception of consciousness is found at the roots of your tree. In the third dimension you create your own reality, which is all that you can see, hear, taste, smell and touch. Your senses dictate what is "real." You have a "real" physical life that is filled with sensations and input given to you through these senses. Your beliefs are formed as a result of your experiences. You see life through the visions perceived through the physical eyes. Words spoken often determine your personal mood. This is the most basic third-dimensional thinking.

In third-dimensional reality, everything that you can touch, taste, smell, see and hear is real, but nothing else. Things you cannot touch, taste, smell, see or hear are not real to you. If I tried to tell a third-dimensional, reality-based person how angels are helping all those who will allow it, he/she might well laugh or want to lock me away because that person would "know" angels are not "real." And if I tried to tell that same person something I could read in his/her palm, I would not be believed because palm reading is silly or evil in that person's world view.

At the most basic level of third-dimensional reality consciousness one sees oneself as a victim of life, helpless to influence it in even the most basic ways. One merely functions and survives. For those who are at this level life on Earth may not be very fun. They see themselves as a feather being blown about on the wind of life. They feel as if they are affected by everyone else's reality.

Most people functioning at this level do not believe in the existence of God because God gives them no "proof." Until they get their proof they cannot believe. A little higher on this third-dimension tree would be the third-dimensional people who accept God's existence. This God is patterned after their "reality"; therefore, God is a person-like being who punishes the bad and rewards the good. This God punishes them when they do something wrong ("I did something wrong; therefore, God burned my house down as punishment"; "I was kind to an old lady; therefore, God allowed me to win the lottery"). They see poverty as a result of a person's bad deeds. This concept of God would be formed from their reality of life as dictated by their third-dimensional reality. Therefore, God would exist as a person-type being who lives in "heaven," which is a wonderful place to visit somewhere just beyond the stars (take a left at Saturn).

At the highest consciousness of third dimension, one would begin to release the need to have a person-type God, and allow a greater variety of form. One would begin to see God as the Creator of diversity and, therefore, diverse in its own existence. But God is still separate from that person. "God, in whatever form, exists outside of me," thinks that person. "I am here and God is in heaven." *It is the separateness that earmarks the third dimension.*

As you move up that tree, you are going to become aware that perhaps there are some things bigger than you are. So you might then be a little interested in some of the things that can't be seen, tasted, touched, heard or smelled--like astrology or psychic phenomena. At the most basic level, you might discount them all. As your awareness opens, you might read the astrology section of the paper, but you wouldn't believe it. Or you might visit a psychic just for the fun of it.

## *Fourth-Dimensional Consciousness*

s you move up the dimensional consciousness tree, you begin to take a little more control of your world. You become aware that you are not just a victim of life, but are instead living in a cause-and-effect world. You become aware that you must take responsibility for your life. This can be a little scary. Many third-dimensional thinkers retreat to the safety and security of the "real" (third-dimensional) world at this point. There, one does not assume responsibility, but can blame the world for one's life challenges. When I asked my spirit friends about the fourth dimension, they said:

> *The fourth dimension is very complicated for the mortal mind to grasp. It is what Eartheans experience in the dream state. It is a dimension beyond the physical; it is of the energy spirits. It is the hearing of what is not there. It is knowing what can't be known. It is what many can already do, but trust it not because it is not "normal." But soon it will be normal. It is the time of great awakening to the vastness of life. It will be a moving beyond the limits of the physical. It is knowing the joy of the angels. It is recognizing your oneness with All-That-Is. It is a glorious time. You are moving into it without struggle or resistance. Let us pray and send Light and Love that those others of Earth shall move into it peacefully.*

When I first received this message, I was looking forward to some strange and mystical world where I would see and hear what wasn't there. Only recently has it dawned on me that I am doing this now. I hear what can't be heard, see what isn't there and know what can't be known, from a traditional viewpoint. That's it--no lightning bolt or major life adjustments. I hear and talk to beings of other dimensions who are not "there" in third-dimensional realities. The fourth dimension was not "out there," but *within me*.

I was somewhat disappointed. I expected a bigger bang. Instead, it was just a widening of realities, much like the poor guy who received a vision of disembodied beings from other worlds "using" the physical bodies of those on Earth. That was the '50s, mind you, and from this vision came the horror movie, "Invasion of the Body Snatchers." I am sure he would be most disappointed to realize that channeling was the intent of the vision and not body snatching, as he envisioned it.

As you move into fourth dimension, you start realizing that there is something bigger than physical existence. You begin to know that there are things that cannot be seen, heard, touched, smelled or tasted and yet still exist. You realize there is a connection between you and other worlds. You begin to look for these other existences. You will find evidence of these other worlds according to your most receptive channel of perception. The three most common senses through which people find proof are hearing, seeing and feeling but not with your eyes, ears and fingers.

*Clairaudience*----------

Clairaudience is the hearing of sounds, music and voices not audible to normal hearing. The French term means "clear hearing." It is not a new phenomenon. Oracles, priests, mystics, shaman, adepts, saints, prophets and holy persons through the ages have recorded occurrences of clairaudient experiences. A few decades ago, if people heard voices, they would be locked away, perhaps forever, because they weren't "normal" or sane. Even that was better than being burned at the stake as a witch, which was a typical punishment just a few hundred years ago. But as more and more people (who also function well in the world) hear disembodied voices, they can no longer all be locked away. Medical science decides whether or not people are sane by their ability to carry on a normal lifestyle. If you function pretty well in your life, but hear voices, the doctors don't worry about it. If you are not functioning well in your life and hear voices, then you will be labeled schizophrenic and given pills.

Clairaudients hear into other dimension. Even this hearing offers options. I have a friend who hears these voices inside her head, whereas another hears the voice from outside her head, as though someone nearby is talking to her. This voice is clearly distinguishable from her own. Socrates, too, claimed to be guided by a spirit friend throughout his life. When sentenced to death, he willingly drank the poison because his guide did not advise him to do otherwise. Several Bible characters, including King Solomon, admitted to hearing voices. And you know what happened to Joan of Arc because of *her* voices.

If you hear voices when no one is around, you can be sure that the experience will knock you out of third-dimensional reality. This definitely makes you aware that the world is really bigger than your personal physical world.

### *Clairvoyance*----------

Clairvoyants "see" into other dimensions. "Clear seeing," or perceiving objects, events or people that cannot be perceived by the physical eye is relatively common. Some people will see all the forms outside themselves, whereas others get an internal vision. Pat Rodegast, who communicates with Emmanuel, tells how she began to have inner visions and feared it was an hallucination. She, like many, was initially frightened by the phenomenon surrounding her spiritual unfoldment. Rodegast sought therapy and joined a spiritual community in her effort to understand what was happening to her. It took two years before she could accept these inner visions. Then Emmanuel, a being of golden light, identified himself clairvoyantly. Together they have produced some insightful books of enlightenment.

The simplest type of clairvoyance is the internal seeing of symbolic images, which must be interpreted. In its highest form, one looks into the various dimensions. During a workshop on spirit communications, one participant was taken to the angelic realms and shown around. Although she had a very difficult time using words to share her experience, it was evident she had a wonderful adventure. People have reported different types of clairvoyance. Some tell of being able to see through things, like envelopes and walls. Some are able to see disease and illness in the body or the aura. Some can see events and/or people that are far away. Still others are able to see beyond time and space.

### *Clairsentience----------*

Clairsentience, or "clear sensing," is a nonphysical sense perception. It is "feeling" the information, a "knowing" through feelings that are beyond the physical. It may come as a fleeting impression, a brief image, intuition or a gut reaction. These may register as internal or external impressions.

An example of clairsentience occurred as I was driving from one of my day care centers to the university where I taught. I suddenly had an overpowering urge to go to a certain fast-food drive-through. I am a vegetarian and I don't drink sodas, so I kept mentally arguing with this message. But as I neared the place, I pulled in and bought a cola. I poured it out as I exited, all the while muttering to myself.

Next, I felt the need to go to my house, which was about three blocks out of the way. (I half expected my house to be burning down as I pulled in the driveway--it wasn't.) I sat in the driveway wondering why I had this feeling. No one was home and I needed nothing from the house, so I left. I was still muttering to myself about the silliness of these feelings, but trusting them too much ever to disobey. As I pulled up to a major intersection enroute to the university, I realized why I needed the delay. A semi-truck and trailer had lost control, wiping out all the cars waiting in the eight-lane intersection. It was a major mess, but I had escaped because of the diversions. I thanked the heavenly messengers.

Another strong knowing came after I had gone to a bank drive-through window. I had processed many transactions which included cashing a check for several hundred dollars. As I pulled out, this strong "count your money" feeling came over me. I immediately pulled over to count it. The teller had not given me the cash! Since I had gone only a few blocks, I returned to the bank, where the transactions were checked and my money was given to me. Another practical application of clairsentience.

For me the experience is similar to intuition, which I have always had, but much stronger. Intuition used to be very light, like a soft idea. This is much stronger and clearer. The more I attend to this knowing, the stronger it gets and the more confident and trusting I become with it.

Clairsentience, clairvoyance and clairaudience are not skills attached to an on/off switch. They are not an either-you-have-them-or-you-don't experience. Instead, they represent a continuum. All of you have these latent skills. If you recognize and use these extra abilities, you will enhance and expand them. Scientists know there are at least thirty-seven ways for the brain to collect data simultaneously. Up to 15,000 impressions can be absorbed at a given instant (Key, 1973). Because the brain can record everything, it must also sort out what is most important for conscious awareness.

Therein is the problem. The conscious mind determines what it will attend to. If it accepts only the reality of sensory information, it validates only that information. Through trust and use, you learn to recognize data gathered from sources outside the five senses. As you trust these extra senses and use them in your life, you strengthen the signals. These skills emerge as you give up the limits of three-dimensional reality. You develop one or all of these abilities as you move up the tree of awareness. By the time you reach the top, you have all three and much, much more.

Things can and do exist beyond what can be seen, touched, heard, tasted and smelled with your physical body. As you move into a fourth-dimensional consciousness, you will know this as your truth.

If you are thinking, "Well, some people can do these ESP things, but not me," then you are still functioning in the third dimension. But it is near the top because you acknowledge the existence of them, though not in *your* life. When you realize that the extrasensory perceptions are available to everyone and you are open to recognize them in your own life, then you will have stepped into fourth-dimensional reality. Proof is required in the third dimension, whereas trust is the basis of the fourth. In order to progress further up the tree of consciousness, you must listen to the inner guidance that comes from these extrasensory perceptions. It is through trusting these new senses that you can begin to experience the natural order of the universe and how it applies to your life.

Keep an attitude of possibility and gratitude as these abilities unfold. They are blessings bestowed on honored recipients when they are ready to receive them. And *you* determine when you are ready. Are you ready?

In the fourth dimension you recognize that life is a play where you are the playwright and casting director. If you have had a terrible mother and an awful father and are tired of that script, you recognize your ability to rewrite it. By changing yourself, you have the power to change everything.

In the fourth dimension you would incorporate love into your script, because you know that unconditional love is the force that allows you to recognize your own power. Recognizing alone allows you a great deal of control. No longer can you say, "Oh, poor me, I just don't have any money this week" or "I don't have..." Instead you ask, "Why did I do that to myself? What is the lesson for me?" When someone really terrible comes into your life, you ask yourself, "What is he/she trying to teach me?" And that changes the whole drama of life tremendously.

This openness, carried to an extreme, helps you realize that all things have a consciousness. I went to Washington, D.C., and parked my car in a parking garage for a week. When I returned to my car, I could feel the car's excitement. It felt like a dog that was so eager to see you at the end of the day that it leapt up and down. The car's energy was bouncing around saying, "Oh, good! I thought I had been left here forever." The car was thrilled that I had come back, and it made me giggle because I could perceive it. It didn't say a word, but its energy was exciting. I have thought differently about my car ever since. While visiting the island of Kauai in Hawaii, the sand "talked" to me, telling me its history and perceptions of modern times. If I'd had less confidence in my sanity, I would have been sure I was insane.

Many children are already aware of the consciousness of all things. They talk about feeling connected with plants and trees and even bees. Certainly, Native Americans were aware of the consciousness of all creation. They acknowledged and appreciated these influences at all times. When you realize everything is conscious, you treat every object or creature with respect. It is not always easy because if you forget to water your plants, you will feel their disappointment. It is now time for humanity to learn from children and from Native American brothers and sisters and begin to allow the consciousness of all things to influence your life. No longer can you take anything for granted.

*Third-dimensional reality is fear- and separation-based, whereas fourth dimension is love- and unity-based.* You recognize that all things are within your power to control and that love brings harmony to all things. It becomes your choice to move into the power of love. If you choose love as the answer to all life challenges, you continue your ascent to the top of the tree. If you don't, you stop your growth at that point until you choose to choose again. The choice is always yours.

Judgments are the basis of third-dimensional reality. You compare your truth to everyone else's. You compare your illusion to everyone else's. You feel pride, goodness, emotional love, hate, anger, frustration and all the other emotions because of these judgments. You realize that all human emotions are the result of judgment. As you move into the fourth dimension, you realize that judgments do not serve you. You begin the process of impersonal living. You begin to observe the process of life without the need to judge or evaluate another. You become aware that you are producing your play and others are living their play. You recognize that because you are so busy with your play, you can't possibly know all the details of another's. You accept this lack of information and do not attempt to judge or direct others. Thus, many of the judgments simply fall away when you move into a fourth-dimensional reality. This process must be complete before you move into the fifth dimension.

In the fourth dimension your concept of God expands. No longer is God someone who punishes or rewards. Now the God Essence cannot be contained within the confines of the old image of God. You realize that the God Essence is a part of you and you are part of the God Essence. You begin to recognize the meaning of this simple fact. But the totality of that truth is not real until you reach fifth dimension.

In the third dimension, you know that everything that is physical is real; everything else is not. In the fourth dimension, you begin to recognize that there is a greater truth. You ponder the meaning of life. You recognize the role of humanity in the universe and the greater truths that exist. You may not know exactly what these truths are, but you are certain that they are not the third-dimensional reality. In the fifth dimension you know, and you know that you know.

You begin to realize that life is a series of choices, and that the choices you make actually impact and create the reality you perceive in physical form. At this point you begin to recognize that you are not your body and can leave it and still exist. You begin to have memories of out-of-body experiences, perhaps during dream states or astral travel. And you begin to see the relationship between the physical, third-dimensional reality and the expanded fourth-dimensional reality. You recognize the power that exists within your soul/spirit.

At the fourth-dimensional level, you still have the illusion of conflict between good and evil and between the forces of light and dark. In third-dimensional reality, you see it as a you-or-them situation; whereas in the fourth dimension, you recognize that the battle is within you. In the fourth-dimensional reality, "light" and "darkness" are provided so you have the opportunity to choose your soul's orientation. You recognize that as you choose your truth, you also impact the greater reality.

You begin to awaken to some of your past-life experiences as part of the greater truth. You begin to understand how these past lives impact your life now. You start breaking the physical bonds by recognizing that the physical body serves you as a vehicle during a limited period, but life and truth embrace a much greater reality that involves many physical existences and many types of beings.

In fourth-dimensional reality, you begin to allow more of the soul/spirit aspect of who you are to have greater input into your physical existence. As you recognize that you are *not* your body or your mind (instead, you *have* a body/mind) and realize that you are something much greater than these, you  empower that greatness. This is the beginning of bringing your physical, mental and spiritual aspects into harmony, which is required to transcend into the next dimensional reality.

In higher realms of the third dimension you might say, "If I think really hard, I can create this." Thus you begin to embrace visualization experiences. In the fourth dimension you realize you *already* create your reality and recognize the danger of third-dimensional visualization. You realize that you have a very limited view of the totality of life. You know that visualizing may actually interfere with your highest good. Thus you begin to trust your higher self, angels, guides and the God Essence to guide your life. You ask for what you want and let them take care of the details because they have the full picture, while you see only a very small portion. You may even say, "Okay, God, You take over; I'm not sure anymore. Let Your will be done." *Surrender of self is your passport into the fifth dimension.*

As on any physical trip, you may return to your starting point many times. So too is your consciousness shift. You may, and probably will, vacillate between third- and fourth-dimensional reality and later fourth- and fifth-dimensional reality until you feel completely safe and make that dimension *your* reality.

# Fifth Dimension

ifth dimension requires total surrender to the God Essence or soul/spirit. Which one of these you surrender to is not important, for the spirit/self is directly connected to the God Source or Light. Light is the universal term for what is referred to as God. Therefore, the act of surrender is significant, for you are relinquishing control to the light, forces of unconditional love and/or higher consciousness. Regardless of the term you use, the process is the same. In this dimension you will learn to harmonize with higher forces, which will have more and more involvement with your daily life.

The fifth dimension brings unconditional love into your daily life.

*Love is indeed something that starts in the universal God presence. It is the glue that keeps all matter together. When you fail to feel love you feel scattered, not yourself. You do feel love at all times, but what you feel and what you could feel is like a blade of grass compared to a California redwood tree. What we are teaching humanity is how to allow love to expand, grow and flourish so it can be the great force it was designed to be. For you see, when you operate in love, no rules are needed...no police, no CIA, etc. For in that energy no one could do anything to hurt or harm another. It would indeed be a beautiful world to live in. But because of the law of free will, it must be each individual's choice--not imposed from someone or somewhere else. Star people/light workers (for indeed they are the same) have chosen to come to Earth to help. You have always been here during the Earth's history, but because of the magnitude of Earth's needs during this time, your numbers have greatly increased and your roles are more important. Because you have come in Earth form, you too must first choose to operate in love before you can assist others to do so.*

Fifth dimension recognizes your unity with the God Essence. This dimension does not accept the concept of a punishing, demanding or rewarding God. Beings here would never "humble" themselves before God, because they recognize that God, in their new understanding, would not find that behavior acceptable. The fifth dimension God Essence is a force that unifies and binds all things together. This God would want humanity to come with heads held high to accept the gifts of abundance from a loving God Source. This Mother/Father/God* would never want or expect subservience or perfection from His/Her/Its* children; rather She/He/It* would want someone with a loving and pure heart who wishes to continue to grow and ascend to higher and higher levels. In the fifth dimension you recognize you are not separate from the God Essence; rather, you are part of the great whole. *All-are-one* in the fifth-dimensional reality.

The God essence is seen as the great Creator who endowed humanity with the ability to co-create. A fifth-dimensional person would never violate this great gift. You recognize that you do not

---

* I realize the She/He/It becomes a little cumbersome but unfortunately we have no gender neutral term. One of my editors suggested I shorten it by combining the first letters of She/He/It and refer to God as shit. I'm sure God would laugh at it but I know a few people who would be incensed. Write me if you have any alternatives to this God/gender dilemma.

have to create with your mind or use visualization to create. Instead, you begin to understand that your creative nature continually creates.

Jesus, the Christ, at the very highest levels of fifth dimension, was able to manifest whatever he wanted instantly because he used his pure, raw creativity and understood how to use these forces in his life. Because those around him operated in the third-dimensional reality, they called them miracles. Their limited reality kept them from seeing that they too could do those things if they believed they could--even though Jesus continually told them they could do all the things He did and more. Jesus told everyone that everything came through him from the Father, who wished all people to have those powers. Those powers, he told them, came through the power of love.

In third-dimensional reality your thoughts, emotions and beliefs determine your actions. As you move into the fourth dimension, you feel a surge of greater wisdom available to you. Decisions are not made based on old beliefs, thoughts or emotions; rather, decisions are made based on intuition (higher knowing) or they are felt in the heart. These decisions are based on your trust in the higher forces and your contact with the source of all wisdom; that contact gives you great confidence. In the fifth dimension your clear sense of knowing is so strong that you would not and could not violate it.

You recognize your need to learn your lessons, because lessons exist in all dimensions and are an important part of the ascension process, which denotes progression into the higher dimension. You also respect other people's need to learn and grow from their own lessons. Therefore, you would never violate their free will or try to force your opinion on someone else. You freely send love to all; you unconditionally love everyone; and you accept their right not to return that love if that be their choice. Love becomes the basis of all relationships. These things, though cognitively understood in fourth dimension, are achieved only in fifth.

Fifth-dimensional consciousness experiences the truth: *All are one*. There is no separation. All pain is your pain; all hurt is your hurt; and what happens to that little puppy on the street also happens to you. You know that all things impact you and you impact all things. Many children who feel the pain of others experience well-meaning, third-dimensional adults telling them they are silly. Those children feel a powerful connection, so it is hard for them to understand how adults can pass by without noticing, feeling or caring.

All groups come together in the fifth dimension. Competition is replaced with cooperation, which creates group harmony. These groups focus on the common good and build on common ground. In the third dimension, group members see differences. In the fifth, commonality is seen.

Relationships are very important in the fifth dimension. Relations are neither personal or emotional, but transpersonal /impersonal. You acknowledge your relationship with all living things--the animal kingdom, the plant world, the mineral kingdom, the Earth, the moon, the air, the oceans, the universe, to name just a few. Native Americans understood and lived this relationship to the fullest.

At this level emotions are put into perspective. One realizes that emotions are often the result of colliding realities and truths, where neither gives way to the other. In the fifth dimension the differing realities blend, each one seeing the other person's views. Understanding, appreciation and respect for the realities of another create harmony, enhancing a relationship. Judgment of another's reality does not exist. This does not imply agreement with another's reality, simply a respect for that person's right to have his/her own unique perspective.

This respect causes you to begin to feel more intimacy in a relationship. You feel closer, thus you experience a truer relationship with all things. In a third- and fourth-dimensional reality, relationships are on an individual, personal life; but from fifth dimension on, relationships come from the spirit. You connect with the spark of divinity within, not from the external, physical self that you see. You bond with all life forms, especially with other people. You recognize and respect the individuality of others and do not attempt to impose conformity. Others perceive your respect and feel closer to you.

You have much less need to defend yourself, even when attacked. There is no need for defensiveness in any form. Each new day is free of barriers and totally open to life. When you are totally vulnerable and open because you *know* that no one can or will harm you because that is your reality, *your vulnerability makes you invincible*. At this level you become much more genuine in your actions and reactions in your everyday relationships. You recognize and allow the vulnerability, seeing it as a very important part of your growth. In fifth dimension you discard all facades, shells or barriers that you erected in third dimension and first recognized in fourth.

If today you need to be defensive, it is because you think there is an enemy out there. In the fifth dimension you would know there are no enemies; therefore, no protection is needed. You know that love is the greatest power known, the first and last defense you will ever need. Third-dimensional love is an emotion--a reaction to something, but at this fifth level you see an impersonal, unconditional love. It is a feeling of connection to, and caring for, all life forms; it thus lacks emotional baggage.

At this level you also begin to understand the process of your higher self and allow it to have input, since it is a larger part of who you are. Your soul/spirit essence is that part of you remaining in spirit form to stay connected to the God Force. As humanity lowered its vibration or "fell away," direct connection to the God Source was lost. The higher self acted as an intermediary. As you begin to recognize and empower the higher self, you increasingly recognize and empower the God Force in your life. Without it the higher self has no purpose. As you continue to do so, you reconnect directly to the God Force through the resulting rise in your frequency.

Eventually you no longer need the higher self; thereafter you reconnect in your own totality of consciousness. (This process is explained more fully in *Many Were Called, Few Were Chosen: The Story of Earth-Based Volunteers* (Harder, 1994). Some people, when they learn to recognize their higher self, choose to take on its identity. It represents an aspect of you, but the totality of you is much greater than the higher self. You have played many roles over many lifetimes, and the higher self is just one, but that was the one in place when you recognized the need to experience separation.

You recognize at this fifth-dimensional level, too, the existence of the extraterrestrials and the contact and involvement with your brothers and sisters of space. You realize that the world is not just this plane, this physical existence, this planet, but is made up of many universes and types of existences. You recognize that there are many forces working on behalf of you and planet Earth. You know Earth is going through a very special, pivotal time in its existence. After asking about why the topic of UFOs is such a secretive one, I was told:

*Because those in power wish to remain in power. If the public became aware of the purpose and the messages of the UFOs, those in power would be forced into either changing their role or losing face. They prefer to deny the existence of extraterrestrial contact. There are those from many worlds who stand ready to assist your planet and its people. They serve the Radiant One and wish to serve all creations of light. They are referred to as the forces of light, also known as the Federation of Worlds. They help maintain the balance of energies on your planet. They ensure that humanity has the ability to choose between the forces of light and those of the lesser light. Those of the lesser light would wish to see humanity remain in fear and controllable through their fear. They do not wish humanity to become free through the process of self-empowerment.*

*All will recognize the differences between them if they choose discernment. No one can interfere with the happenings on Earth except through cooperating with someone in physical embodiment. Therefore, when ones of Earth choose to work in cooperation with the God Force, they empower the forces of light. If they choose fear, separation and/or self-concern, they support the forces of the lesser light.*

There are those beings who work for the good of the planet and those who work for its control and domination. If you tune in to these spirits, their frequencies and energies will enable you to discern whether they are forces of the light or forces of the lesser light.

In third-dimensional reality, many physical "things" are important to you--cars, trucks, homes, whatever. In fifth-dimensional reality, you realize the illusion of believing these things to be "real." But it does not mean that they disappear or that they are not still important in your life. It just means that you are not emotionally hooked on them. If you have a car, that's great. If you don't have a car, that is still great. In fifth dimension you are much more willing to go along with whatever is in your life, whereas in third-dimensional reality you may feel punished or rewarded if you happen to have a few or a lot of "things." At the fifth level you are not caught up in the illusion of things.

At fifth dimension you also begin to see the limitations of illusions as well as the limits and restrictions of spoken language. In third dimension words are helpful to communicate ideas, concepts and meaning. As reality expands to encompass more and more, words become less effective and more confining. In the realms of higher truths and greater realities, language becomes cumbersome and awkward because it cannot communicate accurately. When pure wisdom comes to you from higher realms, it becomes twisted and distorted through language. From this point on, reality must be experienced and not explained, for words will distort it. Your truths are something you know and embrace internally; thus you cannot defend or explain, for they are beyond explanation.

When you reach this level, it is important for you to have direct communication with the spirit world (which is many dimensions beyond our present comprehension), because getting information through someone else is not reliable, as it must pass through that person's limitations in comprehension and language skills. (*Interdimensionally Speaking* by Dr. Heather Anne Harder, a book telling how to achieve this, is scheduled for release in early '94.)

The fifth dimension is a dimension of light and a consciousness of harmony and unity. In this dimension you become aware of the interconnectedness of all of God's creations: the God essence, angels, spirit guides, devas, fairies and spirits of all things. These become a part of your existence. A person at a third-dimensional level may refer to angels, but a fifth-dimensional person knows the *reality* of angels. They frequently ask for and recognize their angelic help in their daily life.

In the third dimension, you know that it is hard to love when you have just been laid off from your job and feel helpless, with nowhere to go. But if these same circumstances occurred while in a fifth dimension consciousness, you would trust the universe to provide. You would understand that a higher purpose is at work and another opportunity for growth is just around the corner. Even in the worst life circumstance you would still radiate love and trust. You would see the blessing in the event, although your third-dimensional friends would think you are crazy.

Making the transition to fifth dimension can be smooth and without difficulty, or it can be just the opposite. All will eventually make the shift, and you may or may not have a choice about making the change now.

*You will help others recognize this higher dimension and allow it into their lives. When enough people on Earth have moved into this higher consciousness, they shall tip the scales and all shall tumble into a higher dimension, much like a seesaw. When enough weight is put on one end, it falls to the ground, causing the weight on the other end to pitch forward. You will provide the "how to" instructions that allow these newer dimensions to manifest into physicality. You understand...many do not.*

This sounds like humanity is going to experience the Hundredth Monkey Phenomenon. In 1952, off the coast of Japan, scientists provided the Macaca fuscata monkey with sweet potatoes, which they dropped in sand. The monkeys liked the potatoes but disliked the sand. A single monkey found she could wash her potatoes in a nearby stream. Others increasingly copied her clever trick between 1952 and 1958. Most monkeys who watched others wash their potatoes also did so, while those not exposed didn't. But in 1958, a strange thing happened. Suddenly, *all* of the Macaca fuscata monkeys--even those on another island a thousand miles away--began washing their sweet potatoes (Watson, 1980). Scientists believe that when "critical" numbers of a species achieves a specific awareness, this new awareness may be communicated mind to mind. Although the exact number will vary, depending on the total number of individuals within the species, the Hundredth Monkey Phenomenon means that when a limited number of people know a new concept, it remains the conscious property of these people alone. But there is a point at which, if only *one more* person adopts this new awareness, the field of consciousness is changed so that this awareness becomes common to the species (Keyes, no copyright).

You are fast approaching a dimensional shift where love replaces fear and unity replaces separation. Each person contributes to the critical mass. Thank you for doing your share.

The Hundredth Monkey Phenomenon also means that even if you are functioning on the third-dimensional level, you may not have a choice about staying there. If enough people move into the fourth and fifth dimensions, you will be "pitched forward" and will be able to see for the first time all those "dead" people you thought were gone. You will hear sounds inaudible to the physical ear. You may be frightened by these phenomena (fear is common in third dimension) unless you become aware and begin to prepare. Begin now by praying and asking for assistance to know the truth. Prayers are always answered.

As you move into the fifth dimension, you recognize that there are no enemies, only a lot of people having lessons, and that if something occurs in your life, it is of your own making. Therefore you embrace that experience rather than defend yourself from it. You allow yourself to be vulnerable, since only through vulnerability do you reach the real power of being.

You also recognize the limitlessness of your existence, and that you really are co-creators with the God force. You create the universe and are unlimited in that creativity and you begin to recognize that there is nothing that is beyond your ability to influence. As it's been said over and over, *Whatever the mind can conceive, it can achieve* (Hill, 1960). It is at this level that the recognized geniuses function when they create those things that seem impossible. They are not limited by third-dimensional or even fourth-dimensional reality, but know that all things are possible. They also, at this level, recognize that all things are energy forms; all things are just pure creation. It is from thoughts that reality is created.

In third-dimensional reality, you think "send love" is just a trite comment. Many times you have heard the advice given in response to queries about how to handle a problem: "Send love. Be love." But at the fifth dimension, you realize the power indicated by these words. When you contemplate love or add love to any situation, you know a miracle-causing process is involved. You begin to recognize the potential for love in every situation, and it is always your choice to expand that love force. You are aware that stress, tension and negativity will restrict that energy, thereby diminishing each experience. You recognize that everything takes us back to love, which is our original source, the universal God Force. As you raise your frequency to all that is pure light/love, you transform your world to one of peace and harmony. The more love you radiate, the more you impact the reality of all people.

Compassion replaces judgment. You no longer feel the need to judge, evaluate or convince others that you are right. You have compassion and understanding for everyone's life experience because you are beginning to understand your own existence. With this comes a whole new meaning and a whole new awareness of who you are. No longer can you identify with the lower self of the ego/personality. The third-dimensional "I am me" feeling of separateness from others is gone. If you ask some of the third-level people, "Who are you?" they would think you are crazy. But at a fifth-dimensional reality, you begin to see yourself not as a human, not as a person, but as a child of the universe, a spark of creation, a part of All-That-Is. You see yourself not as separate, but a blend of the wondrous whole. You develop much more firmness in your belief and stay much more centered, so that you appear stronger. Things that used to irritate you or make you angry no longer bother you. What were obstacles days or weeks ago that prompted great concern are no longer troublesome; the obstacles are more like pebbles.

You begin to love yourself in a truer way and lose yourself in the harmony of the whole. The harmony and the interactions become much more important than your individual existence, which was the reality in the third dimension.

As you begin to understand past lives and how they bring into play the meaning of the whole, you recognize and feel much closer to mastery. Not that you have it at the fifth dimension, but you begin to recognize that it exists, the attributes it has and the steps needed to reach it. Mastery is not considered supreme power, but rather a total understanding and the right use of the universal God Force of which you are a part. Mastery means returning to the essence of who you are and mastering all the processes involved in this lifetime--not for personal use, but for the greater universal God truth.

Until this time you have been veiled from truth and understanding because you couldn't use it properly. You had to be able to experience it and recognize the truth of the totality of existence in order to use your mastery without harm. In third-dimensional reality, it would not have done any good if you had recognized the power that exists, because you would have misused it for your own perceived battles of good versus bad. With your expanded awareness, you no longer have to do battle or feel the separation of opposing forces.

Life becomes more joyous, more harmonious in the fifth dimension. Things are still changing and being altered in your life and on the planet, but they are perceived differently. A life crisis that would have made you an emotional wreck in a previous dimension now simply becomes something you experience, understand, transcend. It does not impact the internal you, and you are still able to feel a sense of joy even when what is happening around you may not appear joyous. Instead of having diminished feeling as you transcend emotionality, you actually *perceive more*.

As you move into the fifth dimension you feel much more and experience much more. It is as though you are taking in more layers of each occurrence: You see them happen at the third dimension, understand them at the fourth dimension and perceive the lessons as part of the whole at the fifth dimension. You recognize your interconnectedness with this, so you literally experience much more from each event or situation. You are not restricted by any one dimension, but can perceive life from many vantage points without resistance or conflict.

At a fifth-dimensional reality, you know that death, too, is a part of life. You recognize the inter-connectedness of the whole, so there is no resistance to that experience even though others call it a "bad" experience. Therefore, you do not have the pain others have from emotional resistance. You flow much more with life and with what is processing around you. You can recognize at any given moment, one person functioning in third-dimensional reality, another person in fourth-dimensional reality, and perhaps another in the fifth, and all of this becomes okay. There is no feeling that you need to make converts, convince them that you are right or that they need to be more like you, because you would see that as a violation of their choice. That would not be acceptable at the fifth level, since you truly respect the place where each person is.

## *Sixth Dimension*

s you travel upwards in your ascension to the sixth dimension, you start tuning in to sounds, symbols and tones. Language becomes less and less important. You begin to recognize the wasted energy that words represent. You talk less and learn more. You conserve every word, thought and action. Reality begins to condense into forms and abstract symbols are packed with meaning. You begin making sounds to yourself. You feel how tones affect your cellular structure as you attune to higher frequencies. You may feel the need to do mantras, chants or tones. They become something you tune in to, becoming a language of the spirit. You may feel drawn to mandalas, symbols or special objects. Words become less and less capable of expressing your knowing; there are no words to express your new truths. These are signals of your journey into the sixth dimension.

In each higher dimension, your former reality becomes more unreal. Your beliefs are laid open for examination and reexamination. Old issues must be processed and brought to closure. Those that were repressed in third dimension rise to the surface again and again until you are forced to deal with and resolve them.

This process reminds me of my childhood. I loved to visit my Aunt Lois and Uncle Gilbert in Tennessee. There were lots of cousins, beautiful country and a cotton farm. I loved summers because I could go there to visit and help in the cotton fields. I helped chop (hoe weeds in the cotton fields) until the cotton was ready for picking. Picking cotton was my favorite chore. I got a long cloth sack about one and a half to two times my body length to hang over my shoulder. I went down each row picking the raw cotton, which came in clumps about the size of half dollar. It took a lot of cotton to fill a bag. Even though cotton is relatively light, the bag became very heavy, and dragging it was an effort. When I decided I was ready, I dragged the sack over to the waiting wagon, where it was weighed and dumped. Then I would go back to chopping cotton.

Processing each new dimension reminds me of those cotton chopping days, with a much lighter bag. Each dimension is relatively easy to enter, but as you do, you have to dump out all your old beliefs. It is your decision, after all. If you don't drop them, the weight of your belief baggage will slow and perhaps halt your progress. The more frequently you are willing to let go, to clear out those old ideas and issues, the easier it becomes to travel through the dimensions. It does not need to be difficult if you allow yourself to dump regularly. This dumping requires the breaking up of old thought forms and brings many strange sensations. I asked my spirit friends about those sensations and was told:

> *They are just another example of growth, which can happen on the inside, outside or in combination. These sensations are a process of inside growth. It is letting go of the old and bringing in the new. Do not concern yourself with them. They shall pass before you know it and a radiant love shall consume you. The old thoughts that bothered you shall never rear their head again. It is the stirring that a caterpillar feels before spinning the cocoon and again before emerging from it. These feelings prepare you for a change. They signal you to pay attention, for something important is about to happen. And indeed it shall.*

As you move into the sixth-dimensional level, you begin to understand why you had to break up old beliefs and why you were unable to use language to express your reality. You realize that at sixth level your language is symbolic. There really isn't a language at all as you define it; there is meaning. These knowings come from color, light, symbols, forms, tones, et cetera. You things in a flash that would take hours to convert to words, if indeed it *know* were even possible to find words to convey the meaning. It's very hard to explain to a third-dimensional person what this dimension is because it is beyond language. It is similar to what happens when you dream and have kaleidoscopic experiences that weave in and out. They made sense to you, but trying to explain them to someone else is impossible. At the sixth-dimensional level exists a reality of symbolism. There are colors and lights and music and exquisite beauty. It is beyond what can be fathomed in third dimension and is hard to describe.

From this point in your journey up the frequency and dimensional tree of life, you must go alone in the physical because no one in physical form can accompany you or share the experience. Much information is currently coming to Earth in an attempt to hasten the ascension of physical reality. These sixth-dimensional messages, although not always understood on this plane, do activate a deep storehouse of information. When you are exposed to sixth-dimensional frequencies via their symbols, they assist you to move more quickly out of third dimension into fourth, or out of fourth into fifth. Earth as a whole is not yet ready for such a pure frequency, but sixth-dimensional frequencies will help you accelerate your own frequency. That's why when some people feel the need to meditate on a symbol, they find that it accelerates their meditation process even though they do not fully comprehend the meaning of the symbol. The mantra, sound, tone, Native American or Egyptian pictogram and crop circle symbol are a few symbols from the sixth dimension. If used properly, these can assist your awakening to higher realities. However, be careful not to create a dependency on any form outside yourself.

Mathematics originated from this sixth dimension. When you truly understand the principles behind mathematics, you are in touch with very great forces. Many people perceive Einstein and others of his intellectual equal as being able to go beyond reality, and they were. It is the reason why he and others broke from traditional view of reality and talked of the importance of things not normally thought about. These people were not born great, but they tuned in and thereby became great. People who reach this level usually choose to disassociate themselves from many "normal" human activities, for those activities no longer serve any purpose. They work solely for the good of all; the individual is of little importance.

Sixth dimension and its symbols are also the basis of understanding numerology and astrology, which are systems that communicate information about various energies through their symbols. Those numerologists and astrologers who are most effective in these professions are able to tap into this dimension even though they may not totally radiate that frequency. If they resist the urge to use this ability exclusively and continue to flow with the universal consciousness, they will reach this dimension quicker than most. Extending your consciousness to that of the sixth dimension requires you to go deeply inward to find an internal understanding. You cannot comprehend the sixth dimension from the outside, although many try, pretending they know. The external world can only give you pieces and teach you specific symbols. But understanding the power of the tones, colors, light frequencies and all else must be an internally guided process.

A friend of mine introduced me to the ancient art of Kofutu. She explained that this was "an ancient system of symbols from the higher consciousness." "This system of spiritual development and meditation uses consciousness symbols to allow communication with higher self and the consciousness of oneness (God-self) with precision, depth and speed. Its use accelerates the knowledge from the unconscious for personal and planetary growth in a spiritual nonego-directed way" says my friend, Carolyn Sheets, who conducts Kofutu workshops. When I asked my spirit friends about them, I was given the following message:

*Yes, those symbols are from the sixth dimension. Many on your planet are more at home there. It is the reason for the upsurge in music, tones, light therapy and, yes, symbols. Just using symbols allows one to feel and experience the energy. Their frequency impacts yours, thereby enhancing you. It is not important to understand or verbalize. Combined with tones or lights, especially bright sunlight, the experience is powerful. They are just another form of Earth therapy being used now on your plane. All combine to make a great mix and support each other without competing.*

*The crop circles are also brought from the sixth dimension for the aid and awakening of your planet. If you meditate on either the crop circles you will develop an understanding of this dimension. You will bring forth the understanding of how these two are related.*

*This is a force field delivered to Earth from the sisters and brothers of the universe.*

Begin to watch for symbolism in the world. Even the practice of Reiki, a form of therapeutic touch, uses symbols to accelerate the healing energy. Symbols are not necessary, but many feel more confident with the symbols and this confidence speeds their process.

It is important to be aware that everything needed for spiritual growth is inside you. There are things that can be purchased that may or may not facilitate this growth. These things may help you focus, attune to different frequencies and in general assist you. This is because Eartheans have evolved to believe that they must have *something* to help, and without these tools they are helpless. Since Eartheans will purchase things anyway, gifts via ideas and inspirations are sent to the planet to assist. BUT THEY ARE NEVER NEEDED! Always what you need is given, provided and contained within. Go within and know the truth.

*You of Earth need much coaching and reassurance. Life is so easy. Yet you let life engulf you...and you allow it. You are standing on the fence. You look at one side, the physical reality of the situation, and feel the feelings. Then you turn your head and recognize the higher purpose of the lesson and the growth opportunities. It is time to move beyond the fence.*

At a fifth-dimensional level, you begin to loosen the hold of your physical bodies, and by the sixth dimension you have altered the physical structure. Your DNA or building blocks of life are permanently altered to reflect a more purified existence, and your body is lighter. This lightness reflects the reduction in density. You don't feel as heavy or as weighted down. This does not imply less mass, as in clothing size, but if you were able to look within the molecular structure of the physical body, you would see that there is literally more space and fewer atoms. You literally create more space within your cellular structure, which allows more of the spirit essence to enter your reality. This is the process of developing your light body.

# Seventh Dimension

In a sixth-dimensional reality, the physical body loses its significance; therefore, for the most part, it does not exist because it is not an important part of reality. In the seventh dimension, you do not have a physical body. The need for physical confinement no longer exists. There are no lessons to learn from the body; therefore it is not used

You do have a unique seventh-dimensional form; perhaps you would call it a pure spirit form or light essence body. It may exist as an expression of an essence of color, sound or tone. The individuality of the entity still exists. In this dimension you are still a separate being with a unique and separate form. Many people have reported visits by entities who have a body composed of light. In this dimensional consciousness you learn your lessons of your unique expression without the confines or limits of physical body. It is a state of connection with Divine Source.

# *Eighth Dimension*

eyond the seventh dimension, there is only the universal, the collective, the mass. There is no longer a specific individual process. You feel the unity because you *are* the unity. Your pulse is the ebb and tide of universal flow.

There is void all around because no form exists or is needed. The sound of the universe rings constantly (which you feel, not hear). This sound is similar to that heard in a large seashell. You experience the flow of the universe in this dimension. You are a part of All-That-Is, but you recognize that there are still new experiences in consciousness. Your consciousness swirls with others like ocean tides. No separation exists, yet you are aware of your influencing presence.

From the eighth dimension individuals choose to come together to create groups which exist as a single manifestation. If you can, imagine a group of friends who are very, very close and who decide to combine units and literally become one essence having the attributes of all the parties. That is sort of what it's like in the eighth dimension and higher. It is a kind of marriage of spirits. Nothing is lost, but only combined; the group synergy creates a much vaster reality. It is the reason that as you move up through the dimensions, the purification of the individual becomes much more important, until at this level the individual is no longer apparent. These groups unify with larger and larger groups. Oftentimes, when communicating with other dimensions, those dimensions will refer to themselves as "we." When asked, "Who is there?" their reply will be, "We are; and we represent a much greater unit."

At one point I wanted to know more about collective consciousness, so I asked my spirit friends to tell me about it. They replied...

*As you grow spiritually, you expand, which allows greater room for the Force. The Force is a collective unit of energy containing all wisdom and awareness. Since you have come for a distinct purpose, you draw into your existence the energy that will assist you in your mission. Each draws in what is needed to the degree allowed. For you see, thoughts of limitations, negativity and fear cause vibrational constriction and the Force is given limited access or even pushed out.*

*You have been given many techniques for enhancing and expanding. You must simply follow the dictates of your heart--not your mind, for the mind analyzes, looks for proof and asks for verification. This indeed limits the Force.*

*You must pray, surrender and allow. Then trust. It works in perfect harmony with the Divine plan.*

Even though this message is referring to a physical expansion, it gives insight as to why those who exist without a physical reality would wish to continue to expand.

These consciousness units grow larger and larger until they represent hundreds of thousands of individual soul/spirits that have combined. Individuals' energies see the need to come together and feel comfortable with losing their identity (seventh dimension) and combining with like consciousnesses to create a greater whole. The ultimate purpose is unification with the God Consciousness in a totality of perception.

# *Ninth Dimension*

In the ninth dimension you have group consciousness coming together en masse to manifest as planets, galaxies, stars or universes, and they create a much greater collective reality so that others may also grow. They combined in the eighth dimension, but in the ninth these combinations grow exponentially and they put themselves in service for the greater good. They see the importance of the greater reality so they offer themselves as an opportunity for growth. At the third-dimensional level, you help, you rescue, you do for others. At fourth, it's unselfish service and helping when asked, but at the ninth, you create opportunities through your own existence for others to grow. You don't force growth, you don't give them a choice and you don't serve. You simply provide a greater opportunity. With our present concept of time and space it is difficult to conceive, yet our planet is just such a unit of consciousness. There is much speculation and certain kinds of evidence to support this theory.

The Gaia hypothesis was proposed by many, but NASA consultant James Lovelock (1979), in his book *Gaia: A New Look at Life on Earth,* brought it to public attention. Lovelock made numerous discoveries that indicated the presence of a self-regulating biological organism. Evidence of this homeostasis: (1) the amount of methane and oxygen in the Earth's atmosphere has remained nearly constant for hundreds of millions of years, despite the fact that methane and oxygen interact to destroy each other; (2) the oceans contain approximately 3.4 percent salt, which percentage remains constant; and (3) the planet has sustained a fairly constant surface temperature despite the fact that the sun is now radiating 25 percent more heat than it did 3.5 billion years ago when life supposedly began on this planet.

This theory has serious ramifications for Earth's pollution problem. Human abuse is throwing this homeostasis out of kilter, jeopardizing the well-being of Gaia. If this pollution were seen as a cancer on the Earth, there would be three possible outcomes: (1) the organism of Gaia will die, taking the cancer and everything else with it; (2) Gaia will restore balance by ridding itself of the cancer and humanity will become extinct; or (3) humanity can begin to function in a symbiotic relationship with Gaia, working in harmony with her. As more people move into higher-level consciousness, they feel the need to attune to the Earth's energies and perform various acts to restore her health. If you feel the need to help, send lots of love and recycle her resources. Gaia, whose name is that of the Greek Earth Mother Goddess, has many stories to tell if you are ready to listen. Are you ready?

Did you ever wonder if a flea realizes his world is a dog's body? Or did you ever see those tiny bugs (too little to see with a naked eye, thank goodness) that reside on the rim of your eyelid? In this ninth-dimensional reality, relationships take on a whole new meaning. Certainly it is time for humanity to awaken to the service and opportunity that Mother Earth provides. It is time to become responsible to and for Mother Earth's well being.

# *Tenth Dimension*

he tenth is really a dimension beyond my comprehension. It is moving beyond the limits of universes. It's the allness, the completeness of all existence. If you compare it to lying on the ground looking at a blade of grass and seeing reality at that level (third dimension), then moving out to the farthest point you can imagine and looking at that same blade of grass, you would see that you lose all concept of separateness. You see such a dynamic, interrelated, intermeshing whole that much of the detail is no longer important and you have become much vaster. The tenth dimension is all-pervading, recognizing all the dimensions. It is pure light. Everything in the universe is in rhythmic consonance. You are the pudding-like substance of all life forms. Yet there is no substance...only ethers. Scent is distinct, yet muted. It is the dimension of everything, yet nothing. You are no longer aware of your uniqueness or anything's uniqueness. All are an equal part of totality. All resonate to the breath of the God Source. The Living Light permeates all with pure bliss.

If you have ever been in a deep meditative state and felt such bliss that nothing else was important; if you have felt your breath was the breath of God, then you may have reached this dimension. In this state you are one with all of creation and nothing else matters.

# *Eleventh and Twelfth Dimensions*

aking that tenth dimension one step further, you'll find the eleventh dimension. This is where you find the God Source. Of course the God Source is the source and the essence of all dimensions, but you experience the purest God Essence at the eleventh dimension. Although you will *recognize* and experience the God Force at the eleventh, it is not until the twelfth dimension that you reunite with All-That-Is. In the eleventh dimension you expand to All-That-Is and become one with all forms and all expressions of all creations. There everything is part of existence and everything beyond that is the Void, which is also the God Essence. Consciousness no longer exists; you experience bliss. The experience is everything there is and it is no-thing.

When in the third dimension, you have your own thoughts, perceptions and reality. But by the twelfth dimension you have given all that up to be a part of the oneness of all existence and a part of the God Source. All individuality, even group identity, is gone. All perceptions are gone. You move into the blissful Void.

This does not represent an end to the process, for the God Force is constantly releasing new sparks of spirit creations to begin the cycle anew. The adventure continues.

********************

As you can see, the descriptions are difficult to put into a third-dimensional vocabulary. If you explore these dimensions within your own consciousness, you might have other experiences and other words. Please feel free to share them with me; but at this point and at my comprehension level, this is the best I can do.

This is a simplistic look at the workings and development of your consciousness. Even in the third-, fourth- and fifth-dimensional levels you will have lessons on many different planets, universes and types of realities. There are infinite choices about where learning can take place within the dimensional realities. The purpose of existence is to experience, learn and ascend through your choices.

There exists no state of perfection that you are to hold yourself to, thinking if you make no mistakes God will be happy with you. God wishes joy and abundance for his creations, and this occurs as you travel upon the path of ascension. It is the *lesson* that is important, and the judgment of self slows your lessons. When you fear the mistakes that may occur you again slow your steps. Release the fear, take risks, then be joyous in the outcome.

> *You still hold yourself to such high standards.*
> *Fear not; humanity is still human.*
> *You are human. Accept your humanity.*
> *Perfection exists only in the movies.*

# *Out on a Limb*

limbing the tree of consciousness can be lots of fun and it offers great adventure. But it is not without some dangers. The tree has many limbs, and there is a tendency to get stuck out on a limb. Each of these branches affords a different perspective. The limb can be comfortable and offer a respite to the weary climber. But be careful; when you get out on one of these limbs, you can get sidetracked from your original spiritual intent of reaching the top.

These limbs may be any psychic or metaphysical experience, like astral travel, tarot cards, psychic readings, channeling, astrology, numerology or any other interesting diversion. The temptation is to become engulfed in an area because of the pleasure it provides. Be careful; it can become addictive. The goal is to continue the climb, not produce more psychics in the world. As you continue your climb you will be able to do all these things and more. Experience, learn the lessons, and grow from the experience. Learn from the lesson, and do keep climbing. There will be a lot of new and exciting things along the way. Do use these things if you feel they help you. They can offer insight and support on your journey. But if you forget there is a journey, then they are not helping but interfering. Don't get stuck out on a limb and forget your journey to the top.

# *Understanding the Mind*

**N**ow that you have a better dimensional understanding, it is time to go back to the mind. The mind is an important player in allowing dimensional shifts. You have allowed your mind to be in control; therefore it is the mind that says, "Yes, you can climb" or "No, you can't." Regardless of what the mind tells you, you usually accept its commands without question, much as young children obey their parents. The child grows up and takes control of his/her own life, but the mind is usually in control forever unless you choose otherwise. For some reason humanity has handed over all power to the mind.

You are not your mind, although you *have* a mind. You are separate from, superior to and much more than you mind. Your mind limits reality based on its beliefs. But *you* are unlimited and without confines.

Your mind determines your abilities. Although the mind has unlimited potential, it is held back by its limited belief system. If you have a third-dimensional reality, you have been told by your mind that you can't do anything except what it tells you. You have put this girdle on your mind by telling it, "Only physical things are real, so I must depend solely on touch, taste, smell, sound and sight!" even though your mind's potential is limitless.

The sheep/goat effect demonstrates this principle: People who believe in the psychic realm score positively in psi tests, whereas those who lack belief score poorly. American parapsychologist Gertrude Schmeidler gave it its name in the 1940s. She postulated that the sheep/goat effect applied to daily life. "People who are relaxed, optimistic and outgoing are more likely to spontaneously experience a wide range of psi phenomena and rely more heavily on intuition. Non-believers are more likely not to have such experiences; if they do, they tend to explain them away as chance, coincidence, or freak occurrences" (Guiley, 1991). Sounds like third-dimensional reality to me.

Learning how to work in harmony with your mind is essential. With this harmony will come an understanding of the mental activation process and the elimination of the constrictions placed on your potential. Believing that another reality is possible becomes necessary for further growth. If you don't *believe* that there is another reality, then for you there won't be.

To move into fourth dimension you must tell your mind to release its constrictions and allow you to explore a wider reality. You have thereby indicated that you want to learn, do and perceive beyond what the five senses tell you. You have given permission for your mind to allow you a greater reality.

# *Subconscious Mind*

The subconscious is the attic of the mind. It holds ALL the memories of this lifetime as well as all past incarnations. It holds the collective memories of all the experiences and lessons that your soul/spirit has had since its inception. Thoughts, memories, and beliefs retire to the subconscious mind when they no longer serve any purpose in the conscious mind.

The subconscious mind contains all the old memories and experiences that are not used in the conscious mind. Every experience is recorded and stored for later access. The subconscious mind is the storehouse of your childhood memories not available for conscious recall; it holds all the memories from this lifetime that the conscious mind feels do not require immediate accessibility. Sometimes experiences can be so traumatic that one chooses to hide them in the mental attic to avoid bumping into them in everyday life. The old cliché that "what you don't know won't hurt you" is unfortunately not true. What lies buried in the subconscious mind often wreaks havoc in your life. Phobias and panic attacks often originate in the subconscious.

The things are quickly forgotten and begin to gather dust. Some people have very tidy mental attics, whereas others are filled with junk and can be quite dangerous. You have access to this attic, but through disuse forgot there is a way to retrieve and use all these old thoughts, lessons and experiences. The dimensional shifts and corresponding frequency changes make it necessary to clean your attic and get rid of some of the old, unwanted and unproductive stuff. The process is not always fun, but it is necessary.

Your conscious mind determines when and how often you are allowed entrance. It feels it is protecting you from your junk. Sometimes it is correct, but sometimes it is not. In order to eliminate the excess baggage and lighten your load, it is necessary to clear out the junk.

The conscious mind must provide access to the subconscious mind. It is never wise to force your way into this area. It is better to bring the conscious mind into harmony with the soul/spirit so that together they can make wise decisions about what is best, as confronting these old experiences, thoughts, memories and beliefs can be quite traumatic.

# *Superconscious Mind*

The superconscious mind is a wondrous depository of everything. It contains vast riches and useless drivel. It contains all the memories of your soul/spirit from the time when you were a spark of the original God force. It contains the knowledge of all souls and spirits. It is a fabulous place to play if you have the wisdom to use the information correctly. Since time exists only in third-dimensional reality, it also contains information on the yesterdays (that really aren't) and the tomorrows (that also really aren't). Psychics tap into this pool of all knowledge when they accurately foretell future events (which is really only probable futures, since there are many futures based on possible behavior choices).

The superconscious mind is the storehouse of all information. It contains the memories of all your past lifetimes, memories of all universes, memories of every lifetime for every soul/spirit. Because all are one, then all originate from the same source. Thus, everyone has potential access to the same information. The superconscious has access, via the subconscious mind, to all abilities, truths and knowledge.

The superconscious mind has been referred to by many names. Carl Jung and Carl Sagan referred to it as the *collective unconscious*. The frequency of the universal mind is the same frequency as the superconscious mind. Thus, when you are able to enter the superconscious mind at will, you have gained access to all knowledge that ever was or ever will be. Whatever you call it, it is a treasure chest that provides great riches to those who are ready to explore and receive the power it provides. But it is not for the timid.

Many tests are given before the doors are thrown open. The entrance exams ensure access only to those who can wisely utilize this information. Only those with a pure heart who can be trusted with the information ever gain admission.

# *Conscious Mind*

The conscious mind has been saved for last because it seems to cause humanity the most grief. Many people are very proud of their quick wit and keen mind. If they only understood the trouble the mind causes, they would not be quite so proud.

Humanity forgot that it had a very wise soul/spirit when the frequency started to fall (Harder, 1994), so the soul/spirit had to put the mind on auto pilot. The mind loved this power and decided it could do more than just maintain the status quo, so it began to acquire more and more power. The saying "power corrupts and absolute power corrupts absolutely" certainly applies to the conscious mind.

Originally, humanity was designed to work in harmony with body, mind and soul/spirit, but the mind didn't like working with a committee. It took control. It decided what the body wanted to eat based on eye appeal, taste or texture, and the body was forced to consume those foods, often knowing they were not in harmony with its needs. The mind made decisions on ethical behavior that violated soul/spirit law. Thus the entity that reflected this mind/body/spirit combination was ever in a personal state of chaos. This internal chaos was reflected in the external world. To restore external harmony to Earth, internal harmony (utilizing cooperation between these aspects) is needed.

Originally, the conscious mind was made gatekeeper of all knowledge. It has remained as the guard who protects you from harm. It also protects you from information and experiences that may inflict pain. The conscious mind allows you access only to facts and experiences in this lifetime that it feels you need, keeping everything else from you. It allows you to know, remember and recall what it feels is safe and/or appropriate, blocking the rest. To dig deeper into the illusion of reality and find truth, you must either receive permission from the conscious mind or remove the conscious mind's ability to block your access.

All thoughts originate in the conscious mind, which puts "safe" information at your beck and call. You can recall and relive many past experiences; you can talk about them if the conscious mind gives you permission. But the conscious mind does not want you to get in trouble, and because it does not have much confidence in your abilities, it blocks access to all but the safest information. Your ability to remember something is directly related to your conscious mind's perception of your ability to handle the information. If the conscious mind wishes you to stay where you are, many thoughts will come to discourage dangerous exploration. These thoughts, once understood, can easily be seen as attempts to control your soul/spirit, but come disguised as safety messages. These thoughts may sound like, "Don't try this; this will get you into trouble. Now leave it alone." If you had a parent/guardian who felt he/she knew how you should live your life, you know how the conscious mind operates. It says (among endless other things):

*Do this.*
*Don't do that.*
*You're going to get in trouble.*
*People will talk.*
*What will people say?*

...and unfortunately you obey without discernment. Listen to your conscious mind and begin to discern its chatter. Listen for the word *should* - it is one of the mind's favorite words. It is often used.

The conscious mind has been given a job, and it does it well. But humanity has forgotten that *it* gave the conscious mind that job. Humanity no longer feels that it has a choice, and as long as no choice is perceived, there *is* no choice. If you recognize that you have a choice, then you can say, "Don't stand in my way. You may not block me. I will do/not do that." When you take charge the conscious mind will begin to assume its rightful place, but don't be surprised if there is a struggle.

The conscious mind is most comfortable functioning in a third-dimensional reality. It relies on the five senses for the facts, but often operates from a fear base. If you begin to recognize the fear behind all the blockages, you will better understand how to work with the conscious mind. It helps if you appreciate the real service the conscious mind does for the totality of you: After all, it keeps from harm all that you are; it builds psychic walls if others try to inflict pain; it guides and controls you until the time you are ready to take command. It has protected you until you are ready to emerge into a world as the child of God that you are.

The conscious mind is a wonderful part of you. Like a guard in a prison, it protects, but it has become intoxicated with power. It no longer feels it must work in cooperation with the body and soul/spirit. Thus to progress up the tree of awareness, you must again bring the mind into harmony with body and soul/spirit. Decisions must be made with an awareness of the totality.

The conscious mind makes decisions based on what it likes, not what is best for the whole. As an example, the mind may want lots of candy because it tastes good, but the body would not choose candy because it recognizes the impact on physical. If you recognize this, you will know when to question the mind, when to question the body and when to question the soul/spirit. If you ask the appropriate aspect questions, you will get wiser answers.

The conscious mind *thinks*, the body *feels* and the soul/spirit *knows*. Pay close attention and listen for these words when you are talking to others. They are an indication of which part of you has the most say in your life. The conscious mind is a great force, and if brought into alignment with body and spirit, it can be tapped for much greater wisdom. If unchecked, the mind becomes a bully demanding, scolding and controlling.

## *Accessing Greater Wisdom by Silencing the Mind*

earning to still the mind is needed before you can bring harmony within. The conscious mind chatters all the time, thus you get used to its noise. When you learn to still the chatter, you will become more aware of the mind and better able to direct it. When the conscious mind is stilled, you are able to gather a much wider pool of information. It is said that Einstein had so many creative ideas while shaving that he would cut himself (Hampden-Turner, 1981). Conscious minds think; superconscious minds create.

To gain access to the superconscious and subconscious areas of the mind, I recommend you begin by saying a prayer and asking for protection and guidance. This will keep you from getting yourself in trouble. I do not recommend forcing entry. Your conscious mind plays an important role in protecting you from very painful experiences. If you force this information when you are not ready, it can do untold damage.

There is a therapist who wanted to "know it all." She went to a hypnotherapist and was put under hypnosis where she recalled some abusive childhood incidents. She has not been able to process these disturbing facts, even though she was trained to teach others to do so. She lost her practice, spent several years in an institution and is generally still very miserable. So, do give the universe the last say in the experience. There are many who know more about what's good for you than you do.

Following the prayer, still your mind by meditation or centering yourself for at least three minutes. Pay attention to your thoughts. Your mind will fight you for control. Talk to it as you would talk to a child whom you love dearly but who has become uncontrollable. Speak with a firm but loving voice, setting limits and defining appropriate behavior. The mind has gotten out of control; now you must firmly and lovingly bring it back to work cooperatively with the body and soul/spirit. After the talk, try again. Keep reassuring the mind that you are in control and that you desire inner harmony. Twice a day sit quietly for three minutes. Insist that your mind be still during these experiences. Thoughts on love, peace, harmony help with the balancing. This is an important step for gaining control.

As you converse with others, watch a movie or have an experience, do not allow the conscious mind to participate. Just experience the now. (We are used to "thinking" and dealing with the mind's distractions, and even coming to believe that all that thinking is good. But take it from a reformed thinker, life is better when you use your mind as it was intended.) Life is much richer when you don't have to accommodate the mind's distractions. There are many books in print that can teach you the skills needed for quieting the mind. Remember that you are not trying to dominate your consciousness; you are trying to harmonize it with other aspects. You must reassure it and relieve its fear. To reach the top of the tree you must make friends with the conscious mind.

As you gain greater control over your conscious mind, you will gain greater access to the subconscious and the superconscious. In the subconscious mind you can access a great deal of information. By continuing the process you can move into the superconscious mind and access *all* information. There you will discover all the wonders of the universe. You can't gain access when rooted in the third dimension because you don't accept the existence of this place of all-knowingness.

Here too, there is perfection in the plan. Access to the superconsciousness is limited to those who have demonstrated integrity and have passed the entrance exams. Even then you do not enter and access the contents like a library. You cannot browse through the shelves until you find a topic of interest. Only when you have a need or a focus are you given access to the information contained. If you are trying to access someone else's soul/spirit record, you will be able to receive the information to the degree that you need it and the other person's soul/spirit allows.

If you have reached the level of evolvement that allows entrance to this resource, you have also reached the point of absolute trust. The information gained is accepted as truth, thus becoming your truth. And when it becomes *your* truth, no one can make you believe otherwise.

To achieve perfect power in consciousness you must recognize the power your mind has for creating your reality; you can begin to use your mind and it's creative abilities so that the one percent of brain usage becomes much higher. You learn to access and utilize a good deal more of your capacities. The more you move up in your awareness and the more belief and trust you have in it, the more you will see miracles happening in your daily life.

The mind has afforded me my greatest personal challenge. I had to loosen its control in my life and bring it into alignment with my body and soul/spirit. The following spirit guidance helped me overcome this mind binder...

*You have many lessons yet to learn. You want so much, yet your mind blocks. You must reassure your mind that it, too, plays a part in the awakening. For without the mind there could be no free will. The mind must see that the soul's path is best. Yet it fears it will become obsolete. It must be assured that it too plays a part. For when one is at-one-ment with the Radiant One, then everything works with perfect love and harmony. The mind will then be at peace and no longer in need of the perfect response or the "right answer." No evaluations, judgments or processing will be needed, for the truth shall be trusted and not questioned by the mortal mind.*

*We do help you, for truly you are a child in the process. You are beginning. You are taking your first step and you feel shaky. This is both natural and healthy. It forces you to move slowly in the vast newness. This allows your cellular body to stay in balance. This balance allows your physical, mental and spiritual bodies to work in harmony. Remember that love and harmony are important. So trust in the greater Divine wisdom that guides your steps, for they are helping you as much as you allow it.*

*Truth reflects the issues. Thought is the process of manipulating truth. Thought creates, conforms, evaluates, judges and applies. Truth simply is. One is a process; one is not. You will work hard on this, for now you do not clearly understand the difference. You are spending much energy thinking about truth. In reality, as you think about truth you are changing it to suit your ego. Truth must be accepted--not analyzed. You have spent many years learning, and then refining your thought process. You have built part of your own reality and identity around thoughts. They have served you well. People will have that much more faith in your trust when you are able to accept truth without analysis. Follow your same process. Accept, relax into it and ask for help.*

*Yes, it does seem strange to discuss the thought process as something to shed in order to know truth. Yet that is what you must do. As you develop your thoughts, you look at things from all angles. You take all sides. Yet truth is one-dimensional. It simply is. As long as you must think, you are evaluating, synthesizing and analyzing. This is an indication of a lack of trust in the information. You shall get to the point that the information given is accepted with a firm mind that knows it is truth. You will not need to quote support, give proof and look at it from various perspectives. You will also be able to share it with the same degree of faith. As you do this, others will also accept it as truth. Until you can do this, others will also feel the difference between a search for truth and the knowledge of it. It will come, because you want it and are willing to release your illusions in exchange for reality. Trust. Know that you move forward in love and protection.*

*Thoughts are your enemy. You must turn off your thoughts, not your mind. You must listen and be silent--*

*but instead, you sleep. There is a difference. You must work on this. Trust in God to help.*

*When you turn inward, you travel back to the time that you were a spark of pure God essence. This trip helps you to remember and reawaken that God Essence part of you. It is important because it allows you to shed the unreal in order to get to the real.*

The above words helped me process some very confusing lessons. I offer them to you with love.

Third-dimensional reality affirms that you are separate from God. "God" is something out there in heaven. As you move up, you can see that the whole purpose of life is to reconnect with God in whatever form you perceive Her/Him/It. God is not only out there, but also *in you*. Therefore, you must be willing to go inward to meet God and in the process connect with yourself and examine your fears. This requires you to transcend the conscious, traverse the subconscious and arrive in the superconscious. It is in this place that you will meet your living God Force, Creator of all and essence of pure light and love. When it is your reality it will be your truth and then you will have all truth.

# *Frequency and Its Relationship to Dimensions and Density*

et us return now to those early science classes where you first learned about the atom and its protons, neutrons and electrons. Do you remember that they were so small you could not see them? And that they were the building blocks of all matter? Good. Now let's build on that. The atom is mostly space, with little particles spinning around a nucleus. It is the spinning that gives the illusion of solid matter. In reality, space is the main ingredient in all things perceived by the physical senses. In fact, I was told that if the space in the human body was reduced by half, a person would fit on the head of a pin. I don't know if this is true, but it is certainly graphic.

To give you an idea of the size of an atom, a single orange, expanded to the size of the Earth, would have atoms the size of a cherry pit. To get an idea of the proportions of the elements of those atoms, if you enlarge the cherry-pit atom until it is up to twenty miles in diameter, the nucleus would be the size of a tennis ball. Its electrons (which circle the nucleus) would be ten miles away. In school textbooks, the electron and the nucleus look about the same size, but in fact, the electron is about 2,000 times smaller than the nucleus. This electron circles the nucleus at 600 miles per second, or 2,160,000 miles per hour (Roger & McWilliams, 1991). It is this speed that creates the illusion of reality that your senses perceive.

As a child, did you ever play with sparklers or a flashlight at night? You could take this single source of light, and by waving it back and forth very fast you could create the illusion of a line of light. Spin it around in circles and you saw a circle of light. There really were no lines or circles, but the rapid movement of the light created what *looked* like lines and circles. It was the movement that created the illusion of a solid form.

Another example of this can be seen by watching a fan. When the fan is off, the blades can be easily seen individually. If you turn the fan to a slow setting, you can still see the blades, but they get a little blurry. Turn up the speed, and instead of seeing individual blades, you now see a solid disk. Turn the speed up as high as it can go, and you no longer see the blades or a disk. Now you see nothing. They seem to have disappeared because of their speed.

If you go back and look inside the nucleus or the electron, you would see that they too are made up of mostly space and something called quarks. Scientists have never seen these tiny bits because they are too small for any instrument but they can determine their nature by their path and behavior. Sometimes quarks, or atomic subparticles, act like particles of matter and sometimes like waves of energy. In fact, if the scientist *thinks* they are matter, they act accordingly. If the scientist *thinks* they are energy waves, then the quarks act like energy waves. Thus, the smallest unit of matter known to scientists responds and conforms to the thoughts of the scientist! You have been told many times that your thoughts create reality. Scientists seem to be discovering the scientific basis for this truth.

This atomic movement also suggests that life is an illusion. If the movement of atoms stopped in the book you are holding, it would cease to exist. If it ceased in the chair you are sitting on, you would fall to the floor. Your mind creates with its thoughts a magnetic type of force that draws these particle waves together to create solid matter. They are not real, only illusion. You can enjoy them and play with them--but don't get hooked on them. As you learn the principles involved in this process, you will become able to instantly manifest anything and everything. This is the universal force, or law, that Christ used when he manifested the fish and loaves.

When I asked what is real, or truth, I was told:

> *Only light, love and God exist.*
> *Everything else is illusion.*

Certainly this is an interesting point to ponder. If you were originally a spark of the God source, then you are real because you are a part of God. God is light and love; thus *you* are light and love. Light and love are real. However, everything created by you is illusion. Illusion can come and go in your life, yet life continues. Your body was a creation; therefore, it is an illusion. Your personality/ego/mind was a creation of your soul/spirit; therefore, it too is illusion. YOU are real, but the things you think real are only illusion. Your thoughts create your illusion; therefore, the illusions in your life are a product of your past thoughts. Your current thoughts will create your future illusions.

Interesting...

# *Frequency*

Your frequency is determined by how fast the atoms in your cells move. This movement is your frequency. Everything and everyone has a frequency that can be perceived and measured. Just as quarks are affected by thoughts, so too is your frequency. Your thoughts determine to a large extent how high (fast) your frequency can go. As you attune yourself mentally to the higher dimensions, you cause your frequency to accelerate.

When you think upon the God Essence, love, peace, harmony and other high-vibrational concepts, you bridge these attributes and the corresponding frequencies. By contrast, when you think about a person who makes you angry or has "wronged" you, when you judge others in your thoughts and/or have other negative thoughts, you lower your frequency. This causes a greater physical density and can make you feel horrible.

Now, I know there are some of you who may think, "Oh, sure!" in disbelief, so I offer the following exercise; (don't believe me, prove it to yourself):

> **Exercise:** First, you will need a friend. Place your palms facing your friend's palms just a few inches apart. Close your eyes and feel his/her energy. When you each can perceive the other's energy, both of you think about the color red (colors carry a frequency, too, and when you think the color you affect your energy accordingly). When you can "feel" red then both of you think green. Feel the shift. Continue to feel orange, blue, yellow, purple, etc.

Each color will feel different. Some people may feel red as heat or intensity or a prickly sensation. It really doesn't matter how it feels; that is determined by your third-dimensional senses. What is important is feeling the shift caused by the change in thought.

If you are willing, both of you think now about someone who really makes you angry (it doesn't have to be the same person). Feel the change. After deliberately bringing on the negativity, undo it by thinking about the color green (which is very healing), contemplating love and/or forgiving that person. Feel the frequency shift again. (It takes two people because it is easier to feel energy changes in someone else.)

The next exercise demonstrates this even further. It shows the relationship between frequency and physical strength. Did you ever wonder why you get so tired on your negative days? Lowering your frequency will wear you out faster. You actually burn 25 percent more energy when you are being negative rather than positive...this does not translate into weight loss, but does cause wear and tear on the body.

**Exercise:** Have a friend place one arm straight out from his/her shoulder. Place your hand over her/his wrist and push downward. Ask the friend to resist your push. Do this to first get an idea of how much strength is in the arm. Now have your friend repeat "I am not worthy" ten times. Then test the arm again. You will both be amazed at how much weaker it is. Those negative words, even though they weren't consciously believed, had quite an impact. Ask your friend to say, "I am important; I am worthy" ten times and test again. Note the difference in strength. This demonstrates how your words impact you--and you use them so casually!

This process is known as kinesiology, or muscle testing. It is fun to play with and can be used in lots of ways to see if things are good for you (when your strength is unchanged or increased) or not so good for you (when your strength is diminished). Try it with food, vitamins, even clothes. It is amazing how it works. It is another source of *weird and wonderful* information. The following exercise can be done at your next party or gathering. It will astonish your friends and make you become more aware of your thoughts. It clearly demonstrates how your casual negative words or thoughts impact others as well as yourself.

**Exercise:** First, test the strength of two people, using the above method. Then send them to another area so they cannot hear you. Select one of the two people and have everyone in the room think negative thoughts about that person. Be sure to select someone who can handle the negativity.

Bring the people back into the room and test their strength again. Be sure these two people stand at least six feet apart when you test their strength because the negativity of one can and will impact the other. The person sent negative thoughts will have much less strength than he/she originally had, whereas the other will be unaffected. After you demonstrate that one is affected and the other isn't, have them stand shoulder to shoulder and then demonstrate how the nearness reduces the strength of the second one.

Next, have the group undo their negative thoughts and replace them with loving ones. Test their strength again. Both will have increased in strength, and the person who had received the negative thoughts will be back to normal.

Each thought creates a thought form. Each thought goes out into the universe and either helps (raises) or hurts (lowers) the collective consciousness on Mother Earth. Each thought will come back to the sender because of the *law of return*. This law is also referred to as the law of cause and effect. Simply put, it ensures that what you cause, you will also feel. So before you finish this exercise, you may want to ask the angels to dissipate any negative thought forms you may have created in your past so they can't damage anyone. If you have also found yourself having negative thoughts, ask the angels to dissolve them and help you recognize and move beyond the need for any negative thinking.

A third-dimensional person may laugh at this suggestion, but humor me. Your thoughts *do* have forms not visible to you. If not altered, even these experimental negative thoughts can affect the universe and you. So why risk it? The angelic forces stand ready to assist humanity. Ask them to assist you with any task at hand, and you will be amazed at how much easier life becomes. Now that you have seen the impact of the negativity of other people, I'm sure you will not want to be affected. Here are some ways of protecting yourself from the negativity of others. I call this my *cosmic condom*. Don't leave home without one.

**Cosmic Condom #1:** Surround yourself with the radiant light of the universe. This can be done by declaring you are protected, by seeing yourself enveloped in a blanket of light or thinking/feeling yourself protected by the light. Light has a very high frequency and the lower frequencies cannot penetrate it; therefore you are protected. It is like trying to throw a marble through the spinning fan blades. The marble cannot make it through the spaces because of the speed of the fan, so it bounces off. Thus negativity is bounced off your protective light.

**Cosmic Condom #2:** You can say or think, "I am protected from all but the highest and best," and ask for "my highest and best good, as well as the highest and best for all concerned." You can also ask the same for the universe. This is a mouthful, but it is a phrase that covers all areas and is very effective. These things can be said out loud or in your head. Your words and thoughts create your reality; therefore as soon as you say the words or think the thought, the deed is done. Testing your strength before and after will verify the reality of its protection. Think about this the next time you are beating yourself up and saying negative or uncomplimentary things about yourself. Even in jest the words have power. Select them with care.

If you are entertaining the idea of sending negative thoughts to your enemies, forget it. If you had tested the group in the earlier exercise, you would find out that when they began to think negative thoughts, they too were zapped. Their strength was weakened just as the object of their thoughts had been. "What you sow is what you reap" holds true even when it comes to thoughts.

The goal is to get your frequency as high as possible, and thoughts play a major role in the process. There is no contest; God does not give out medals to the first ten winners. All are encouraged to accelerate their frequencies. The more you help others, the more you help yourself.

There are many things in your world that affect your frequency. This was made very clear to me one day as I received the following message (I had been thinking very specifically about one spirit friend prior to receiving it):

*Yes, I am near. You see, when you think or speak of another you bring their energy into your own. So your thoughts draw me to your side. It is also the reason why the news, either in print or video, serves you not. For it draws into you the negativity on your planet. Pray for the news and the newsmakers, for they shall pass from this plane. They do not accurately reflect the happenings of your planet. Rather, they create a reality that some of your planet wish to create. Send them love and surround their news with love as it goes out into the consciousness of your planet. Ask us on the other side to empower that love. Ask for the audience to have discernment. This shall help the situation. But it is best for you to spend that time contemplating joy and love. If the news lost its audience it would exist no more.*

I have often felt depressed after watching and/or reading the news; now I know why. I was also told to keep the microwave and the television unplugged when not in use, as they are programmed with a frequency that lowers your vibrational level and makes you more controllable. Weird but interesting!

As you raise your frequency, all of your physical perceptions are expanded, allowing your range of perceptions to widen. As an example, your vision allows you to see tunes in a certain range of frequencies. Scientists know that there are frequencies both above and below this range that are out of our visual perception field. In fact, what you can visually perceive is actually a very, very small part of what exists. As you alter your own frequency, you also alter your ability to perceive a wider range of frequencies. As you increase your frequency you will see spirit forms of those people who have passed over (many children can do this now); you will be able to see the auric energy field of people (some can already do this); and you will be able to see more colors of the spectrum.

The same applies to hearing. There is a normal range of sounds which most humans can hear; yet you know that sounds occur both above and below this audible range. Dogs hear and respond to the sound of a whistle humans cannot hear. Elephants are known to communicate at a sound range below the range of human hearing. This was discovered when someone *felt* that very low vibration. Sure enough, the existence of the sounds could be verified with instruments even though they were inaudible to humans.

As the frequency of your body changes, so too does your ability to perceive reality. Your reality thus changes, which in turn affects your consciousness. As your dimensional consciousness changes, so does your frequency. Thus, each boosts the other. This synergy makes it easier to abandon the belief that reality is limited to what can be touched, tasted, smelled, seen and heard through your physical senses. The speed and ease with which you come to terms with this expanded reality is the same degree of ease you move from one dimension to the next. Some people move very easily, whereas others wrestle with what is "real" for a long time.

This expanded reality took on new meaning as I began experiencing several dimensions simultaneously. This is what was told to me:

*Life will get more complicated. Remember, we told you. You are beginning to operate at many levels simultaneously. That is why you can have an experience and be outside the experience at the same time. You are doing fine. You are understanding the experience as it happens. Do not concern yourself with details. Just experience the now and "let go and let God!" You are in good hands. You speak of trust, yet you hold onto the threads. You still need a sense of control. This will pass as your life gets too deep for mental interference. And it will. It is why you "hear" many voices--the main one and the echoes around it that interpret and enhance. If you did not learn to handle many tracks--like your eight-track players--you could not keep up with the energy that you are being given. You must relax into the experience. Soon you will be having more complexity in your life. This too must be accepted with joy; and isn't joy wonderful? Just wait; bliss is just around the corner. When you finally accept bliss, it will blow your socks off. You are getting close. You have followed directions well. All is in Divine order.*

Nothing is ever lost as you increase your frequency and climb the dimensional tree. Everything simply expands, and the perspective through which you view the world shifts. Negativity and limitations are no longer important and cease to exist in your life; few would recognize this as a loss.

The God Essence has a frequency of pure, unconditional love. Every dimension below that gradually slows the rate. As you move up the tree of dimensional consciousness, your frequency must be raised in order to continue the ascension. This is a cause-and-effect relationship, but it is impossible to determine which is the cause and which is the effect because they are interchangeable. The frequency can affect the dimensional reality and the dimensional reality can affect the frequency--like the chicken and the egg (which has been argued for eons and no one yet agrees which comes first). Rather than trying to decide which is the more important or the "cause," let us just say they are both important and affect each other. To get to the top of your dimensional consciousness tree, you must continually raise your frequency and be willing to shift your reality.

## *Physical Density*

The physical density of the human body is determined by its frequency. The body is affected by everything--thoughts, words, beliefs, food, drink, breath, exercise, dimensional reality and the frequencies of others. As humanity lifts its eyes to see new and higher dimensional realities, human bodies automatically increase their frequency and lower their density. The body undergoes physical alterations to accommodate these density changes. Sometimes there is some discomfort involved with these alterations and humanity takes a pill to stop the symptoms. The whole wondrous process is thereby brought to a screeching halt; progress stops due to a lack of understanding.

It is imperative that you see the connection between frequency, density and the body. This will allow you to work with the process without blocking it and medication does block it, even well meaning over-the-counter medication.

Density refers to the condition of the physical structure. In third-dimensional reality, the physical structure is very dense. It will seem heavy and compact, much like your discomfort after consuming a large, heavy meal; because you get used to this feeling, you think it is normal. As the body changes its frequency you get strange feelings due to the density shifts, and you think that is abnormal. In truth, it is the body attempting to revert to its natural state.

When I asked what I should convey to you about this process, the following message was received:

*Your message must be one of preparation: how to prepare oneself for the approaching new age. You will outline the physical, spiritual and mental steps that must be taken. It will contain the changes that will or may occur. Then tell them how to best deal with these personal changes. The topic of elimination may not be a pleasant one, but understanding cellular cleansing is important, and you shall discuss it with dignity. For one cannot make the ascent to the new vibrational frequency without altering the body. Therefore, the process must be made public and open for discussion...or those on your planet will continue to reach for a product that will cure the "ailment" and thereby stop the process.*

If your dimensional consciousness and your frequency are to move beyond the limits of the third, then an understanding of the expected physical changes is necessary. The physical body must be harmonious with your new and higher frequencies. It must cleanse each cell to rise to and maintain this frequency. The body, mind and soul/spirit must always be in harmony if you are to arrive at the top of the tree.

The following message was given, explaining the importance of this melding of the body, mind and soul/spirit. It also tells of the rewards if you are successful.

*You can easily accomplish any task in pure (spirit) form, but you must do it in the physical. This is the difficult part. This is the reason why the lessons and help are given on a regular basis. It is the physical mind and body which are being altered; your spirit essence needs no preparation. So, much of the physical process must work together; the body, mind and soul must meld with the God essence/spirit/force. This is your process. When you accomplish this, you can be the right hand of God to help those who also choose love's path.*

The problem is, you don't always get in tune with your body. Your mind, not your body, usually determines what and when you eat. Your mind chooses when you exercise or when you play. Your body suffers because of it. When the body is not happy and in good shape, you feel awful and less energetic. Your spiritual progress can be slowed or even blocked. Humanity needs to first learn to attune to the physical body, recognize the great role that it plays in life and then begin to listen to the recommendations it gives.

As you learn to make friends with your body, you will also become prepared for some of the changes that may/can/will take place. I say may/can/will because each physical structure is different; therefore, different cleansing processes will be needed. No two bodies are exactly alike, therefore, no two cleansing and aligning processes will be exactly alike. You must listen to and attune to your body for guidance.

## *You Are Not Your Body*

The idea of making friends with your body may seem foreign to you, but it is a necessary step if you are to make the ascent. The body is an entity separate from you. YOU ARE NOT YOUR BODY. You do *use* the body. You have a body and you are served by the body.

The physical structure plays a major role during your lifetime. When it is healthy and in good repair, it certainly impacts the quality of life you have while on Earth. Therefore, it is important to learn to live in harmony with it. Yet it is important to know that your body is not who or what you are. When your body has an ache, it is not *your* ache. That pain belongs to the body. When the body dies, you still exist. The body, much like a car, is the vehicle you use to get around in while on Earth. If you have ever been plagued with a car that has a multitude of problems, you begin to realize how important it is to keep your physical vehicle happy and in good repair.

Over time, you will choose a new car, and so, too, with the physical. You periodically get new ones--one new body per lifetime. (There are some exceptions to that, but we'll save that discussion for another book.) Just as you select your car, you select and help create the body you will occupy during this Earth walk. I am sure I have lost a few third-dimensional people with that statement. I can hear you saying, "No *way*! I would never select *this* body!" Yes, dear friend, you *did* select that body. You had your reasons, which in your conscious, third-dimensional state you do not recall. Usually those reasons relate to previous life experiences.

I know that although my body changes from one life to another, my identity did not. Remembering my past lives caused me to know that I am not my body. I recalled various lives as male, female, pretty, homely, tall and short, but always I knew it was me. My body and life circumstances changed, but I did not. Often the physical encasement became like a costume in a play. In order for the play to be more believable, I had to dress the part.

During one quiet meditative experience, I had memories of selecting my current body prior to coming into this lifetime. My body is okay, but few women would ever knowingly choose it. I remember saying, "I want something sturdy and healthy." I remember selecting a body with no waistline, rounded features and rather nondescript. I did not want a body that would distract me from my work nor one that would cause me to worry that men were after me just for my physical beauty. (My husband assures me that I have nothing to worry about.) I can remember other lifetimes when I was gorgeous, and it was a pain in the neck.

Amazingly, during all the physical alterations that have occurred during this ascension process, I have altered and greatly reduced my food intake. Sometimes I did not eat for a week at a time, yet my body has not dropped a pound or altered an inch. I know that if the purpose serves me, my body will adjust. But for now, it remains just as I chose it--healthy and sturdy. And I *know* that I am not my body.

The body, like the brain, is a marvelous apparatus. One of its main functions is to retain emotional memory. If during one lifetime you were injured, then you carry the scar to this day. When you stuff emotional hurts, either in past or present lifetimes, your body pays the price. Tears are a very effective way to release the emotional trauma of the experience, but we will get into that later.

## *Making Friends with Your Body*

It is time to meet your body. I know you know about your body, but have you ever talked to it like a supportive friend-- like it too has feelings? Probably not; well, it is time.

> **Exercise:** One approach is to close your eyes and see your body as an animal. Call the animal to you. Watch it. How does it feel? What is its condition? Listen to it as it communicates with you either mind-to-mind or with words. Ask it questions. What would it like you to do differently, better, et cetera? Allow the experience to unfold. Don't try to force a message. Just relax and allow. If you have badly abused the body, it may take a while for it to trust you enough to communicate.

I was introduced to this exercise by my physical therapist after a car accident. My body came to me as a poor, mangy, overweight, pathetic-looking deer. Its hair was falling out in spots and it looked terrible. I felt so bad, all I could do was laugh and apologize to this poor deer. When I asked what I could do to make amends after all the years of neglect and abuse, it replied, "Just love me."

It was true, I hadn't cared about the body and in many ways felt it was a bother. In an article written much earlier, I had written that the body was the "robotic covering which gives the brain the ability to carry out body functions to ensure the brain's health and longevity. The body is a structure that ensures that the brain can protect and propagate itself; like the skin of a snake that is shed, the form is altered and left behind in the cycle of human life." As I read that now I think how cold that was; nonetheless, it was how I felt at that time.

After meeting my body, my attitude toward it changed. I started doing things just to make it feel good. I took long, soaking baths. Eventually I got a hot tub, and I sat in the warm water and told my feet how much I appreciated them for carrying me around each day. Each part of the body was shown appreciation and love. I, the total me, felt much better. No exercise was needed, just a little TLC.

I have conducted that exercise at many workshops. Each person gets messages and impressions that are different. Each person's body seems to have very distinct needs and is grateful when the person cares enough to listen.

After I got to know my body and gave it permission to give me messages, my diet began to change. The changes were slight at first; then greater and greater shifts were made. Eventually, I used a treadmill for awhile. I walked approximately thirty minutes a day (still no weight reduction). I stopped using the treadmill when I no longer felt it was needed. I have great energy and I have a better relationship with my body. I also know that I need to always be working in harmony with my body if I am to ascend to the higher dimensions while in the physical. It isn't difficult or unpleasant, and the rewards are wonderful; all I must do is listen to my body and respond to its requests.

## *Role of the Physical Body*

esides the storage of emotion, the body has many interesting functions. I was told about many of them so I would learn to appreciate the physical structure. As you make friends with your body, you learn other things. For instance, the nasal passage contains an essence that holds you in the reality of time and space. It is one of the reasons you often breathe in through your nose and out through your mouth as you prepare for meditation. This process causes the unifying of third dimension with infinity. When you have a head cold and breathe through your mouth for awhile, you begin to feel disoriented--out of touch with reality. If you breathe rapidly through your mouth you will hyperventilate, or disengage from time and space. Carried to an extreme, you will pass out or vacate the body. Your body does not enjoy this experience, so don't do it just for fun.

Your body does not really need food. Rather, your body is designed to eat because the jaws contain an etheric pump that cleanses the etheric and astral bodies as you chew. The more you chew, the more cleansing occurs. This pump acts like the heart by causing a circulation of energies that facilitates the cleansing. As the human diet became soft and less chewing was needed, chewing gum was given to our planet to make us use our jaws more.

If you would learn to breathe properly. you would be able to pull "essence" out of the air to nourish the body. The breathing I was taught is a hissing breath. As you breathe in deeply, your nose makes a hissing sound. Hold it for a slow count of four, then release it from your mouth on a slow count of eight. Try three of these in the morning as you wake up and feel the stimulation. If you haven't been breathing properly, you will have accumulated some junk in your lungs, so don't be surprised if you find yourself coughing throughout the day. Don't try to suppress the cough; work with it to clear the lungs. When I asked about a friend's cough, this was the explanation given:

> *She is clearing her lungs for the new breath; when one breathes the ethers, which is different from air, one uses a different lung process. She has for long periods used her lungs improperly; now they must be cleared out for the new. Tell her to resist not. Instead, cough deeply; this will speed up the process. Suppressing the cough causes the need to continue. She should get the phlegm from the base of her lungs. She will find herself breathing differently, deeper and less frequently. All is in Divine order.*

Have you ever watched people sit around and rub an ankle or wrist? A *tamorrhea* is placed on the body, usually on a wrist or ankle, at birth. This is an etheric ID band, which contains all of that soul's historical information as well as the soul's purpose during this lifetime. As it is rubbed, it activates the memory. It is one of the reasons many people are drawn to wear ankle or wrist bracelets; they, too, stimulate the tamorrhea and activate the knowing.

I could go on and on, for every part of the body is built by design for Divine purpose. The more you become friends with it, the more it will share its many secrets with you.

# *General Body Changes*

n the beginning, your body did not have physical form. The light body, or body of light, allowed you the freedom to interact in many planes, in many universes. It allowed you to move in and out of any form you wished to take. You could raise the frequency, thus reducing its density, or lower its frequency, increasing its density. Things happened that changed all of that (explained further in *Many Were Called, Few Were Chosen: The Story of the Earth-Based Volunteers*, Harder, 1994). Over time, the physical body became more and more dense. It lost the ability to change frequency and alter density. In fact, it lost the ability to do almost anything except live. The physical body is a girdle of sorts that you put on when you enter into physicality and take off as you exit. Like a girdle, it is confining and restrictive. The ascension of consciousness allows you to transform the body back to the light-body existence of times long ago. The ascension is all about expanding the limits of physicality. It is the physical body which is being expanded.

To facilitate this physical ascension and the acceleration of frequencies, the body must be purified. This cellular cleansing occurs over time to prevent great physical damage. If it occurred all at once, it would impact the cellular structure much like very high notes impact a glass goblet--it would shatter. The safest process is a stepping-up procedure. Each step requires you to take a certain action, which brings certain results. As you refine your body so it can carry the very high frequencies, you are taught the ability to also lower the frequency at will, thereby again allowing you the choice of form.

This is the ability used when Jesus and other great masters appeared and disappeared at will.

Do not force yourself to do a thing because you feel you must. If an action is in cooperation with the body and is spirit guided, it will be easy. No sacrifice is needed. Sometimes it will require you to create new habits, but once you see how much better you feel, these habits will be easy to maintain. By the same token, do not avoid doing something because it seems strange or because you fear people will think you a fool.

Never follow the advice of a friend when they tell you what you must/mustn't or should/shouldn't do. It may be right for them and be their truth, but it may not be yours. Nor do you need to follow the arbitrary dictates of a book. There are some companies that promote their produces as "transformational tools." By all means check them out and then follow your guidance. You must learn to listen to your body and your internal guidance. No two physical bodies are the same; therefore, no two purifications are the same. Tune in to yours and listen. Take all external advice and pass it through your filter of internal discernment. Trust what comes.

Having said that, I will share with you many of the bodily changes that I went through. Some were stranger than others. Some had unusual physical symptoms. All increased my frequency. Some you may experience; some you may not. I experienced symptoms like everyone else, and had to trust the process. Afterward I would ask my spirit friends about the symptoms. I always checked with them before I saw a doctor or took medication. Often I would pretend to take medication to make my family happy. My spirit friends would explain what was happening, but always after the fact. I, too, had to go through the experience veiled.

I am not suggesting that you fail to seek professional help if you feel the need, or stop taking medication that may be prescribed to you. I am telling you to listen to your body and inner guidance to ascertain the best step for you. We live in a commercial-filled world that preaches that an external product will cure you. If we listen to the body, it will tell us whether a product, patience or procedure may be in your best interest. Do listen to your body to discover whether it needs outside intervention. Listen to your internal guidance before you reach for the "product that will cure the ailment," thereby stopping the progress.

## *Water*----------

As my frequency accelerated so did my intake of water. I was told that this allows each cell to feel the frequency more clearly by increasing its resonance. The increase in water also helps the cells hold a higher frequency and flushes away the old cells. This flushing is necessary because each cell has an individual frequency range, with its predetermined high and low. In order for the cell to extend this range old cells must be constantly replaced with new ones. The new cells are then able to extend ever higher with their frequency. Water helps to flush out the system, washing away these old cells.

Your body's main ingredient is water. Scientists tell you that you must drink eight glasses (eight ounces) each day just to flush out your physical system. Your body will only release the same amount of liquid as you drink. Therefore, if you drink only two glasses of water per day, then only one-fourth of your body fluids are cleansed. The other three-fourths are the old, stale, impure liquids that are filled with old yuck (This is an unpleasant thought, isn't it?). It is important that the water be clear water (as opposed to tea, coffee, juice, flavored water or water and lemon) since any flavored water must be filtered through your body as a food and does not have the same cleansing abilities.

Consequently, drinking water is important just to maintain your health, but as you go through the frequency acceleration process you will need even more water. I found that I would often drink up to a gallon or more per day. If you can imagine this process as being like changing the oil in your car, you will begin to see how important the water truly is. Now there is great debate over bottled or tap water. Unfortunately, I can't provide you with the *right* answer because there isn't one. In the end there is just a choice. According to my spirit friends when water is taken out of circulation, as it is when it is bottled, the living life force contained in the water dies and is not as good for the body even though it may be purer. On the other hand, tap water often contains unhealthy levels of chemicals and heavy metals. So in the end you must decide which is the best choice for you. Regardless of your choice, water is always better for you if it is blessed as this greatly increases the frequency of the water.

There are several techniques for blessing your water. All of them are very easy. First, you can send the water light and love. This can be done by seeing it as in a vision, saying it or just trusting that your thoughts have created this as your reality. You can say, "I bless this water" (out loud or silently). You can ask God and/or the angels to bless the water or fill it with love. Any of these techniques are equally effective.

In fact, if you would like to test the effectiveness of these techniques, here is a simply test. First, take a drink of water. Really taste it and see how it feels in your mouth. Next, use one of the above techniques to raise the frequency of the water. Now taste it again. Can you tell a difference? Most people can. Some say it is sweeter, clearer or even seems softer in their mouth. You have actually changed the molecular makeup of the water. If you feel really scientific, you can also do this to food. Take two dishes of food, fill one with love and then let them both rot. They will rot differently. The blessed one will last longer than the unblessed dish. It is a fun activity for children! They love to watch food spoil.

If you want to experience the ultimate in super powered water then you might want to experience *mineral tea*. It is easy to make and carries a very high vibration which your body will respond to very quickly. Take a clean rose quartz, amethyst, or clear quartz crystal and place it in a jug of blessed water. Place the water containing the crystal in the sun for a minimum of twenty minutes. Drink it sparingly, perhaps a few glasses per day. This treatment really accelerates the body's frequency, so be prepared for the side effects.

There are books available on making gem elixirs. I do suggest you buy one before you begin experimenting with your own varieties of mineral tea, as some stones can be toxic. The three stones I mentioned are always safe to play with. The rose quartz accelerates the love frequency, the amethyst is a sonic purifier and the quartz crystal amplifies. If you drink too much mineral tea it will have the same type effect as drinking lots of caffeine, you will get extremely wired. Some people even experience accelerated diarrhea.

## *Diarrhea*----------

This is such a big part of the transformation process that I decided it needed its own category. I have mentioned it in several places throughout the book but now I will have a serious conversation concerning this process. (My spirit friends have assured me that it is possible to discuss this topic with dignity so please support me and don't act silly.)

As I said earlier, the water will help wash away all the old lower frequency cells. These vacate your body very quickly once they have been discarded. This is a very powerful and important cleansing. We have been programmed by television commercials to believe that loose stools are something distasteful and unhealthy; therefore there are many products on the market to help alleviate these unpleasant symptoms. Be warned when you reach for the product that stops the symptoms, you also stop the progress.

Back in my days of being a university professor, I taught a graduate nutrition class. In my research for that class, I learned that when the physical body is perfectly nutritioned, the bowel movements will be the consistency of mashed potatoes, the mustard colored and odor free. This is very similar to the stools of a breast-fed baby. For most adults, our bodies are way off base on these elimination guidelines.

I have talked to many people who indicated they, too, have had these changes in their stools. Use it as an indication that the body is reverting to a healthier status. Unfortunately, you may have a tendency to reach for medication when your stools get loose. Please resist it, for this is one of the most important processes needed for the frequency acceleration.

Allowing diarrhea is a very important process for that light body you keep hearing about. As you shed the old, slower vibrational cells, not all of them are replaced. Thus your body becomes less dense in physical matter or lighter. Your complexion becomes more flushed and takes on a ruddier look. Because there are literally less cells in your skin, it takes on a transparent look. Eventually, your skin will take on a translucent quality which allows your light or soul to shine through. I call this a spiritual glow. As your body develops this etheric essence you feel better and more healthy.

Always ask yourself "How do I feel?" before determining whether you need to medically intervene with your diarrhea. With harmful or nonproductive diarrhea you will become listless and dehydrated. In general, *during* and *after* the cleansing bouts you feel awful. With the spiritual cellular purging you may not feel great *during* (there were times I recited the Lord's Prayer over and over just to get through it) but *after* you feel wonderful. You are more energized, lighter and happier. People will often comment on how good you look, the weight you have lost, or your new hair style. Even though none of these are true (I haven't lost an ounce of weight nor an inch of body bulk during all of this), they do perceive something is different but do not know how to recognize nor express the difference. So instead they comment on the things that usually change people's appearance.

## *Diet*--------

Your diet will be adjusted to bring in the elements needed, as well as eliminate those that do not serve the physical you. The diet will change quickly, so don't stock up on a favorite food. For two weeks I dined almost exclusively on avocado and sprout sandwiches. I wanted nothing else then, but it's been over a year and I haven't had one since. I have never been a big eater of sweets, but for several months I needed a weekly Hershey's almond candy bar. When you attune to your body it will gently guide you to what and how much you need. Listen to its messages.

As my frequency accelerated, I gradually eliminated all meat, including seafood, from my diet. My system now cannot tolerate either. Even meat drippings in a soup base causes great discomfort. Any meat consumption causes a severe, 24-hour flu-like disorder. I cannot even physically touch meat and even find myself blessing the meat counter as I pass it in the stores. These reactions are due to the very low frequency of the meat. Meat is not bad, but the callous, disrespectful way we handle and care for our animals fills their frequency with fear and unhappiness. Therefore, when you eat meat or seafood, via the animal flesh, it lowers your vibrations. As my frequency rose, meat was not in harmony with my body. Meat was not hard to give it up; I found myself simply wanting other things. There was never a struggle or sacrifice with any of my dietary changes. I simply listen to my body.

For awhile my milk intake increased. Now I haven't had any in months. Sometimes I eat lots of eggs--then during some periods, none. I find myself eating much smaller portions and at very strange intervals. I do not eat at mealtimes but rather when my body tells me it wants to eat, and then I feed it what it wants.

This is also helping to prepare me for possible times when food will be scarce. With all the talk about Earth changes, I once asked if I should start to store or stock up on food. I can now laugh at the idea because what I would have stored then I probably wouldn't eat now. My spirit friends once asked me, *"Could you really eat, knowing others were hungry?"* I knew I couldn't and it was the last it was ever discussed. As they explained. . .

> *There will be a time when food on this planet is scarce;*
> *therefore it is important that humanity not be tied to*
> *the conventions of man. Your body does not need*
> *nourishment three times a day. It is best to break the*
> *habit now. Follow your inner guidance, not rituals.*

This message was a great help in learning to eat only when my body required food, which was not nearly as often as I had been eating. I told my dear family that they were on their own from that moment on. Food would be in the house, but I would no longer prepare meals. Since I had never been a Betty Crocker type homemaker, it didn't come as a great shock. My children are older teenagers and they are very capable of fixing their own meals. I do have to admit, I felt very guilty and neglectful for awhile, but I have finally gotten over it.

As I began my spiritual path, I greatly increased my consumption of raw fruits and vegetables. I do eat some cooked, but I much prefer them fresh. I am told that it is even better if you can grow your own. Since all things carry the frequency of its creator, food that is grown and cared for in love carries a higher frequency than other similar food. Food which you grow yourself will also carry an energy much more harmonious to your own. If you can't grow your own, try to buy produce locally grown by friendly and loving people. It really makes a difference. I can now tell by the way my body feels when I eat a carrot with an attitude or an unhappy cucumber. I intentionally select happy and contented food and my body is grateful. Regardless of the food you purchase, blessing it prior to eating it really helps the process.

Be aware that sugar greatly slows your frequency. After a extremely intense workshop, sometimes I will use sugar to ground me if I feel I have accelerated too quickly. However, in general, if you want to increase your frequency, it is best to eliminate sugar from your diet.

Caffeine has the same effect as sugar. I no longer have any desire to drink anything with caffeine, including tea. I just don't like the way it makes me feel.

For awhile I felt the need to drink Jason Winters herbal tea. I felt fresher and less dense after drinking it, so I asked about that.

*The tea is helping your development. It is a gentle cleanser and assists in washing away the impurities from your cells. This allows greater light force to enter. The effects are subtle, but you can feel the shifts. Taken each day, especially in the morning, it would be most helpful.*

I used it regularly for awhile, but just as suddenly as I had felt the need to drink it, the feeling left. A canister of it has been sitting in my cabinet for months.

A friend wanted to serve Sunrider tea at a spirit communication workshop I was giving. My spirit friends had said only water or pure fruit juice were to be served, so I asked them about the tea. Since this workshop requires participants to accelerate their frequency so that spirit contact can be made, I did not want to do anything that would interfere with this process. This is what they said...

*It would assist others to drink the tea prior to the workshop more than during it. The tea should be consumed ceremoniously morning and evenings the week before. Blessings should be sought for self and tea as it is consumed. It is best to see (visualize) it as a gentle cleanser that lovingly moves through each cell. This process is much like cleaning house before having guests. You are preparing the way for the light source.*

Alcohol is extremely quick-acting. It lowers one's frequency even before the liquid gets to the bottom of your stomach. It occurs so quickly that it creates a type of energy/frequency vacuum and even lowers the frequency of those around the person drinking. If you are around someone who has been drinking, surround yourself with light which can protect you from their alcohol. This will prevent their frequency from affecting yours. A little alcohol can impact you as much as a lot.

Your diet may/can/will see many alterations--from one week to another, from one month to another and from one year to another. So don't plan on working out a perfect diet plan and staying with it for the rest of your life. As your body changes, so will its needs. Stay receptive to those needs. As your diet starts to shift, be prepared for well-meaning friends who fear for your health. They will push meat at you and insist you eat it. When I explain that my body has developed an intolerance for meat and it literally makes me sick, they leave me alone. If they still push, I offer to take a bite and throw up for them. This usually ends the discussion.

You will be able to tell when your body is in good health. Learn to trust your body and your inner guidance. Well meaning people will tell you what they think you need to be healthy, but it is your body that is the expert on what you need. We have each used different techniques to screw up our body; therefore we will each need to do different things to heal it. There is no book out there that has given me the steps to health that I have had to follow and I have read many. Always it has been necessary for me to listen to my body and respond accordingly. When people try to warn me about how I am destroying my health with such a weird diet (which it is), I offer to match them with energy, strength, stamina, and general well being. Thus far few can match my wonderfully hectic and demanding schedule.

The diet that I have consumed over the last several years would make any dietitian's hair turn gray. It follows no principle that science teaches us. It has no consistency. But with each bite I feel better and more in harmony within. If I live on popcorn for a week and a half, then I know that is what my body needs. When I taught my graduate nutrition courses I confidently told my students, who were teachers themselves, what they *should* eat and what they *need* to teach their students. I believed it when I taught it, but I am glad I have not been asked to teach that class after my beliefs changed. Now, I could never dictate the *correct* eating patterns to others, knowing how wonderful the body is at directing the best individual path.

In the end only you can determine if you are healthy. Do you feel good? Do you have adequate energy, or are you listless and tired all the time? As you move through the spiritual frequency ascension you will have many body adjustments which bring upon specific physical sensations which will not be pleasant, but you will always feel a joy and an inner knowing that these bring progress. It is vital that you learn to listen to your body.

## *Wardrobe----------*

This has had an interesting affect on my wardrobe. I can also tell the frequency of the clothes I buy and wear. I have had to have the angels clear some of my old clothes in order to even wear them because of their frequency. When I buy new clothes, I first feel the frequency to see if I can even wear them. Along with the frequency of the garment, I also check the fabric contents. It seems I have developed an intolerance for most synthetic fabrics.

## *Sleep----------*

My sleep patterns vary greatly. There are times when I need very little sleep; one or two hours a night and I am fine. There are other times when I need fourteen or more hours per day. If I am processing a lot of new energy, I may sleep lots or very little. Again let me suggest that you listen and follow your body. If it needs rest, give it rest. If it doesn't, then stay up and do something productive. Don't complain that you can't sleep; be grateful for the extra hours. Complaining slows your frequency and gratitude accelerates it. You are always making choices that help or hurt your development.

Don't try to sleep when you don't need it, and don't try to make yourself keep going when you obviously need rest. During the week I spent in Egypt my energy was incredible. I slept very little during that week, perhaps ten hours total. When I got back I could not stay awake. I slept almost round the clock for several days.

The body is very wise and knows how to keep itself healthy; pay attention to its signals. I find it amazing and a little sad that most people have accepted the belief that they need eight hours of sleep per night just because some experts at some time told them they did. Now is time to take control of your own body, in cooperation with your body. It alone can tell you exactly how and what you need. Learn to listen to your own personal inner expert.

# *Energy Infusions*

There are many types of energy rays being sent to this planet at this time. This planetary energy infusion is being sent from various sources for various reasons. These energies are neither good nor bad, they simply are. They do, however, have a strong impact on humanity. They are causing an acceleration of the planet. This speeding up process is being felt by all and labeled by some as the *quickening*. Have you noticed that everything in your life seems condensed? Does life appear to be accelerating? If so, you are feeling the effect of this energy.

This energy also magnifies and intensifies everything in your life. If your life was a little crazy last year, then it's a lot crazier now. If your life was great last year, then it is even better now but much faster paced.

This energy is also resurrecting old issues you thought were buried and forgotten. This can be a powerful clearing energy if you allow it. It seems to force you into dealing with old issues. Remember the clearing out of the subconscious mind? Well...this is it. This energy is forcing you to take action. Rather than grumble about the crazy life you have (which lowers your frequency), look at the things causing the craziness. Examine the lessons that are becoming apparent and deal with them. Let go of all the things that do not serve you, whether they be physical or emotional. (If you have difficulty letting go I do recommend *Exploring Life's Last Frontier: The World of Death, Dying and Letting Go,* Harder, 1994, as it has many helpful lessons on letting go.)

Clearing out the old junk is always a prerequisite when moving from one house to another. You are making a very real move, from the old, dense, perhaps unhappy physical structure to a light body. All of the old emotional garbage holds you to a lower vibrational frequency. After you complete the process you will be happy you put in the effort to release the garbage. It is not an easy process; sometimes it borders on miserable. But it is a *doable* process, and the end results are well worth the effort. When I was clearing out my old garbage, I was told...

*Yes, you listen and you are confused. But fear not; think not; feel not; just exist in the moment. This is a now and you should experience it, but don't become bogged down by it.*

*You shall experience a great many new or extreme experiences because you are asking for release. Just as air bubbles must rise to the top of boiling water, so too must these experiences rise to your consciousness. They are present in an altered form when the water boils not, but they go unnoticed. Your life is beginning to boil, so much must be released into the ethers. You are doing well. We have said many times to relax into the experience. Let go and let God. Why do you not? Why do you feel YOU must do it? Have you never wanted a partner that does the work while you reap the benefits? That is God--and you know He/She/It exists. So let your Partner do the work. You have struggled long enough.*

*You have many lessons yet to learn. You wish to rush; yet in the rushing you might miss some of the beauty. You would also blur the process. You must know the process because others will ask. You must not only give the answers with words, but with your life.*

Imagine an energy scale of one to ten. One is the weakest energy and ten is the strongest that humanity can handle. From January 1989 to about March 1990, Earth was sent "2" energy. From March 1990 until December 1991, it received "3" energy. In January 1992, "4" energy was sent; it reverted to "3," where it will stay until the 23rd through the 26th of July 1992. At that time we will be sent a "7" energy. By January, 1994 we will be receiving "8.5" to "9" energy. People need to be prepared physically, spiritually and mentally. Depending on how that energy is processed, more or less energy will be sent. You make the determination. You help decide how fast the acceleration of energy of Earth will occur.

This energy is causing all humanity to make choices. No longer can you be undecided about light, love and the God Essence. It is time to decide which team you are going to play on--the forces of light or those of the lesser light. The Bible talks about the time of separating the sheep from the goats and the wheat from the chaff. Well, this is that time spoken of so long ago. No longer can you play both sides. If you choose the forces of light, be prepared for lots of personal energy infusion. If you choose those of the lesser light, I don't know what will happen; but I am sure it will bring you a series of lessons, and eventually you will be able to make a new decision.

## *Processing the Energy*

here are many ways to best utilize this wonderful energy. It is wise to remember that the energy magnifies where you are at the moment of infusion, so begin by consciously keeping yourself in the place of center. Much like a lump of clay on a pottery wheel, when the wheel spins the more centered the clay is and the less you notice the speed. In fact, if the clay is perfectly centered, it appears not to move at all. If the clay is off center, it can spin wildly and even fly off the wheel altogether.

Your thoughts, words and actions are always your choice. If these are of a high vibrational nature when the energy comes in, then these will be enhanced and expanded and thus your frequency will be raised with very little trauma. If you are holding on to old emotional hurts or buried issues, or if your thoughts, words and actions are of a lower vibrational nature, then these too are magnified and enhanced in your life. You will then have to go through more difficulties in order to incorporate the higher frequencies into your life. Your outward vibrational realities (trauma, discomfort and pain) are reflections of your internal state and are not dependent upon a harmonious external situation. In your place of center, you exist only in harmony and everything is in balance. The more time you spend in your center, the more calm and serene you become. You may still have outward challenges in your life, but you will handle them in a peaceful manner. Regardless of life circumstances, you must take charge of your life and keep your reality clutter-free.

**Find your center:** Finding your place of center is much more difficult sounding than it really is to do. To find your center simply *intend* to do so. Your thoughts and words make it so. It is a vibrational state that connects you to Divine Source. To first learn to recognize it, I suggest that you close your eyes and think yourself there. It will be a little (not much) more peaceful, a little more tranquil, a little bit calmer. You will feel a slight shift of energy when you move to your center. I often refer to your center as your phone booth. Just like Clark Kent had to go to his phone booth in order to turn into Superman, you, too, must go to your phone booth to become all that you can be. Your phone booth is your place of center. Some people have created elaborate scenes of woods, beaches, mountains as their place of center. Others have made it a room like a family room, office or library, and this is fine, too. Whatever makes you most comfortable is what is best for you. I have always had just a wonderful sense of void, a state of being that is much like a womb where I can go to find a Divine connection. There I feel nurtured and am able to regain my own equilibrium when life becomes demanding. Over time I have learned to carry my center with me so that I am ever in my place of stillness and my source of strength.

**Deal with the issues as they arise:** Always it will be much easier for you to process these new energies when you are in your center. Also you can best process and gain the most from the new energies by dealing with your present and past issues, not suppressing or avoiding them. This is similar to sorting through a pile of old papers that you have been avoiding or saving. It is best to make a final decision on each sheet of paper as it comes to you. That way you can decide in the moment: does the sheet serve you and deserve to be kept, or is it to be discarded? If you decide to keep it, it is best to be filed in that same moment rather than added to a new pile. In doing this you will never have to again deal with those papers. But if you simply move the papers around from one pile to another, then you will continue to be bothered by their presence.

*Learn to play:* The energy intensifies any situation, so learn to lighten up. Play and laugh at situations and feelings. You may have a feeling of urgency or importance. Do whatever your guidance dictates, and do it with a light heart. Playing is a vital part of spiritual growth and is seldom give its due reward.

*Ask for assistance and guidance:* Trust that you will get the guidance that you need if you ask for it. Then follow that guidance. This sounds easy, but it is not. Many times as you are swallowed up by life's challenges, you forget to ask for help until life becomes overwhelming. You think you are unworthy (thus don't expect the God Essence to bother to reply), so when the wee, small voice does speak, you don't recognize or acknowledge its presence. The God Force doesn't speak with a megaphone. Guidance comes through hunches, intuition, feelings and/or thoughts. Only after you trust this inner voice are you able to get information in words, writing and speech (there are exceptions to this). When you get these feelings, act on them. Don't wait for a notarized letter from God to follow your inner guidance. Remember, inner guidance is from *within*. It is *your* guidance; therefore it will feel like you. But if you accept that you are a part of the God Source, a spark of pure essence, then you will recognize that you are a pretty great source of guidance. Not your mind or your body--the guidance must come from YOU, the soul/spirit aspect of the greater you--the you that is connected to the God Source.

*Sing:* I found singing to be very beneficial in balancing these new energies. Singing seemed to spread the energy evenly (at least as I perceived it) throughout my body and loosened up whatever was stuck. Sometimes I would hum, tone, chant and even whistle if I felt like it. All seemed to be equally helpful. The song didn't seem to be consistent. Whatever I felt like singing was what I used. My personal favorite is "The Battle Hymn of the Republic". I am told that it was given to humanity to eliminate fear. It does seem to brings courage and dissipates lower frequencies. "The Lord's Prayer", "Twenty-first Psalm" and "Amazing Grace" are also very powerful. I do recommend that you not sing just any song; find one to which you feel connected. Find a song that brings joy, or peace, or harmony or trust or courage. As you begin to feel the songs, you will learn to recognize which ones bring on which attributes, and you will develop a whole songbook full of personal favorites. Trust your knowing.

***Get into nature:*** I have also found holding plants, walking on the grass and touching any form of stones or rocks to be helpful balancing tools. Mother Earth is also being affected by these increased energies, and when you use her to help balance yourself, you are also balancing her. You are helping with her healing, for which she is very grateful.

As each person learns to find balance in an increasingly off-balance world, the process of balancing the world is assisted. Each of you will be given the help you need to always be in your place of center and power, if you are but open and receptive to it. It may not always make sense, but it will always work. Do not judge what your inner guidance dictates, but do open yourself to the experience. If it makes you feel more peaceful and in touch with the greater cosmic reality, then at least give it a try.

# *Personal Energy Infusion*

s you indicate your desire to grow physically, mentally and spiritually, there are those on the other side who will assist you with the process. I imagine it to be somewhat like an intravenous tube etherically attached to you. There is a constant infusion of energy which speeds and accelerates your vibrational frequency. At specific times great amounts of this cosmic life force are injected into your totality. I seem to have gotten most of my big injections in the middle of the night, as have many of the people to whom I have spoken. Since I am very energy-sensitive, I could feel the shift of vibration even in my sleep and it would immediately wake me up. Sometimes it was a challenge to get to the bathroom in time for the cleansing which would always occur. Sometimes there was slight nausea; always there was diarrhea. The diarrhea was the shedding of the old--getting rid of the lower frequency and cleaning out the body. It wasn't always comfortable, but it was always a giant step forward. It wasn't fun at the time, but hours afterward I would feel much lighter.

**Balancing the energy:** Twice I received *very* heavy energy infusions. The first time it occurred, I could feel myself going into a rage. I stomped and screamed, yelled and threw things. Internally, I felt like I had gone insane and had lost all control over myself. My family reacted with shock and told me how crazy I was acting (as if I wasn't aware). Even though I agreed, I was helpless to stop my behavior. I said and did all sorts of things I am not proud of, and it took about twenty-four hours for these feelings to subside. When I finally calmed down, I asked my spirit friends what had happened. They explained that these personal energy infusions are usually monitored, but the person who was to watch my monitor had stepped away from his/her job. The accelerated energy had caused me to get out of balance (remember the pottery wheel). If it ever happens again, they advised me to get away from people (I am still apologizing for some of the things I said) and **demand** that my monitor be checked and my energy immediately be balanced. Everything went well for a month or so. Then one day I felt this rage begin to return. It took me about thirty minutes to recognize it and demand that *"somebody get to the controls and check me out."* If it was from an infusion, I wanted to be monitored and kept in balance. I could feel the change (slight) immediately and within 15 minutes I was back to normal. I was told it had been a test to see if I would remember to ask for balance, and I would need to remember those situations so I could tell others about them.

# Specific Body Changes

With the many physical alterations that were being made on/in my body, there were also physical sensations. I prefer not to refer to them as aches and pains, although on many occasions I could not tell the difference. I have always enjoyed a relatively healthy and pain-free existence, so I wasn't used to these irritations. Because I knew they were a part of my acceleration process, I never became very bothered with them (there were a few exceptions). Also I always knew that when the symptoms were over, I would get an explanation, for I, too, had to go through these experiences without fully understanding what and why they were occurring. I offer some of my experiences as a possible explanation of your own. As always I suggest you learn to listen, follow and trust your own inner guidance as to what action, if any, is required.

## *Ears*----------

When I first began my vibrational ascent, I would often hear a ringing or bell-like tone in my ears. I asked if there was anything special I should do when I heard that sound.

> *No. Just listen and give notice. The sounds are coming more frequently. You have paid attention to each; this is good. You are a good listener. Many continue to ignore the signal. The signals will get louder, more intense, longer. Soon words will follow. Do not be alarmed. It is just a more direct form of communication. But it can be frightening for many, so this is the best way to begin.*

The ear sensations did not last long at any one time but they did become more and more frequent. I would always silently acknowledge that I heard the tone. In my imagination I saw a little man conducting a test on my circuitry and figured it would help him to know if he had made the connection. I am not sure how long it has been since I last heard the tones, but it has been a long while. Even though my interdimensional communication process continues to evolve, I am not receiving voice transmissions in my head...yet anyway!

## *Tears*----------

It may seem hard to believe, but tears are one of the most powerful physical cleansing agents, second only to diarrhea. Like diarrhea they are difficult to stop once they start. Diarrhea cleanses the old unwanted cells and tears clear away all the old unwanted emotion that has long been stored in the cellular structure.

Tears are very healing. I found myself crying a lot as I moved through the various emotional storage spots throughout my body. I went through boxes of tissue to process all the saved-up emotion. Sometimes I would know what I was crying about, but sometimes I didn't. The tears were always the sobbing-type tears, and I always felt much better and lighter afterward. It was similar to the early stages of pregnancy when the hormones are going crazy and one cries over nothing. Most of the time I avoided people during these teary stages. I just couldn't explain that I was crying over something that happened perhaps 500 years ago. By the way, the next time someone tells you, "There is no use crying over spilled milk," tell them I said they were wrong. If that spilled milk causes strong emotions that you stuff or suppress, it is better to cry now and get it out than never to cry at all.

Before you complete your ascent up the dimensional levels, you, too, will probably have to clear out all those stuffed emotions. If you are continuing to stuff, be prepared for some major tearful cleansing.

Now as I help other people move through some of their lessons, I am not surprised when their tears spring from nowhere. I even feel elated because they are allowing themselves to let go of old emotional issues. The more you have stuffed, the more tears you will shed.

My crying was intense but like everything else it too faded into my past as I found more joy in the now. If you are moving into this phase of release, the best advice I can offer is, *"This too shall pass."*

## *Body Temperature*----------

I have always had a tendency to be on the cold side, which I had attributed to low blood pressure. But as my body went through various cycles, I found lots and lots of extremes. Sometimes I would be very cold; nothing would warm me up. This, I was told, was caused by the lowering of my metabolism, which was necessary to activate a certain type of energy within my body. Sure enough, like the diarrhea, when these cold spells were over I would feel improved.

Other times I would be very hot--like hot flashes, although I can't be sure because I have never knowingly had one. One time the heat was so intense that I called on Jesus to hold my hand until it passed. He did, explaining that this was necessary to burn off impurities. It wasn't fun but it was fast, lasting only several minutes.

On one occasion my temperature changed from one extreme to another (chills and fever). It lasted for nearly twenty-four hours. I spent the time in bed and later asked about it. I was told...

*It was a cleansing and refinement. You literally burned off the "less than highest"--that was the heat. Then you endured the cold--this eliminated more. The process continued until the portion of your brain that deals with the "needed capacity" was activated. We realize it didn't feel good--but it was good that you endured it without medication. The brain is sometimes sluggish from long lack of use and must be given a jump start, much as you worked your car door lock several times before it would work properly. This is unfortunate, but there is no other way. You handle it well. You will feel the mild throb for a few more days, then you shall begin to notice the change in your vision. This will be the first of many small steps. Do ask us and we shall explain, for you will need to tell others. It will be a small sacrifice for what you will gain.*

Amazingly, I did notice the change in my vision. It got worse. Things became fuzzier. I did change the prescription on my glasses several times but nothing seemed to help. I was told that this was one of the side effects of seeing beyond the third dimension (or physical reality). According to my friends as we begin to move beyond the physical plane all the definition of space will begin to fade. I can't say that I enjoy fuzzy vision.

## *Heart Sensations*----------

Over a period of weeks I began to get stronger and stronger sensations in my heart area. I didn't take any chances with that one; I had some medical tests, which showed nothing abnormal. They continued to get stronger until one day I asked my spirit friends about it. They replied...

> *Your sensations of heart constriction is from a shifting of the heart chakra. As you know, the heart chakra is off center.* (Actually, I didn't know this.) *This is the result of generations of lopsided thinking, downward energy shifts and being closed off to much that would help. Yours is being centered and adjusted to prepare for the additional influx of love energy to flow through. This cannot occur in a single period; the physical body could not handle that. Therefore, the process occurs in stages. This is your third adjustment. There will be five given in total. Each one will last several days and cause mild to moderate sensations of discomfort. We would rate what you are feeling now as mild. They are nothing to concern yourself with and, like everything, will assist with your growth.*

I discovered their rating scale is not the same as mine. What they referred to as mild, I classified as moderate to severe. I don't go to the doctor frequently--perhaps every couple of years. This time I had went in for tests right away. But the above description did match my sensations. It did feel like my heart was being dragged from left to center. I had never thought before about the heart and heart chakra being so closely linked, but this communication certainly made it sound like they are one and the same. For those of you who may not have been exposed to the term *"chakra"* before, chakras are the energy vortexes that penetrate the physical and auric bodies and through which various energies, including the universal life force, are received, transformed and distributed.

As we, and the Earth, are moved into fifth-dimensional reality, the heart chakra is vital to carry this energy. It took several weeks for the major sensations to subside and several months for the minor sensations to cease. After this process was complete, I could tell a great difference in my energy level and my general feeling of well being. They were right as usual.

## *Headaches*----------

As I told you earlier, I have a sturdy and healthy body; I have not been bothered with lots of aches and pains. Therefore, these strange headaches caught my attention. They were never exactly alike. I have referred to them as headaches but I now prefer to call them head sensations. *Ache* has such unpleasant connotations where *sensation* is a more neutral term.

One type of head sensation was a piercing throb right between the eyes. It didn't last long (several hours) but it was quite severe. I was told that this was the activation of the third eye. An etheric wedge had been inserted to complete the opening. That certainly describes the physical sensation.

Another head sensation was located at the base of my head where the spine enters the skull. This area, at both sides of the brain stem, had a sharp to dull pain. Pain wasn't the only strange thing: This area began to grow. I now have a large bump on each side of my head. The last time I got my hair done, my beautician asked if I had injured myself, so I know it is not my imagination. This, I was told, was caused by the activation of my *"communication center."* This facilitates my communication with other dimensions and life forms...weird. Even though most of the other head sensations have long stopped, this area continues to itch, much like a wound that is beginning to heal.

Another head sensation started just above my right ear and each throb would move up and over my head until it reached my left ear. The throb would then jump back to the area above my right ear and start again. This lasted for about ten minutes per session. Perhaps there were four or five sessions.

There were many other strange head sensations; usually they were intense, but for a relatively short duration--never like a typical headache. Each one was part of the process of activating some dormant part of the brain, I was told. You may or may not have headaches; they may or may not be similar to mine. The important thing is to listen to your body and find out what action should be taken. A well-intentioned aspirin can stop your progress and leave your brain in the same dormant condition. Eventually if you are to break through your physical limitations, you must endure and overcome these sensations.

The typical advice given to me was to breathe deeply and slowly, relax my body and move *into* the experience. I was told not to resist the experience because that accelerated the pain. If it were severe I might be told to lie down. All of these things helped, but none of these things made all of the sensations go away. I was once told that I could take a "pill" but should be aware it would slow the progress. I didn't take the medication.

### *Stomach Pains*----------

I had some incredible stomach pains, nearly as strong as during childbirth. I was told it was due to a chakra block caused by a trauma. The body was holding on to the energy rather than allowing it to flow. It took several hours, but I finally released the experience. It turned out to be a past-life-trauma caused when I was viciously murdered, Jack-the-Ripper style. The emotional trauma of the experience had been stored in my stomach, blocking the chakra. I cried for days over the experience. Once I recognized and allowed the experience, the pain was gone. One does not need to recall an experience, but at that time my mind had to know everything.

As you begin to tune into your source of discomfort you will also begin the process of healing. Pain is always the result of holding on. As you locate pain in your physical structure, and search for the meaning and lesson it brings, you will begin the letting go process. I even got to the point where I looked forward to the pain because I knew it signaled a new level of growth as I learned to work with the discomfort.

I cannot tell you what to do to release all that you need to release, but I can tell you the secret is to move into the experience and not to resist. Total surrender to the moment brings the quickest and most harmonious frequency acceleration.

## *Limp*----------

One day I found myself walking with a limp. I don't recall any pain, but the limp was real. When I asked about it, I was told I was resisting the experience. When I recognized how I was *"dragging my feet,"* the limp disappeared--another example of allowing the experience to unfold. Always there is a lesson nestled inside the experience.

## *Skin Rash*----------

Upon returning from a trip I broke out in a terrible skin rash that covered my torso and legs. The bumps were about the size of dimes and itched intensely. I tried everything to get rid of them. My spirit friends told me it was the *"manifestation of the last of physical-life irritation"* and they told me to *"move into the experience."* I understood the words but I did not know how to "move into" a rash. I pondered this for days...moving into a rash. Meanwhile I tried everything to heal my rash to no avail.

I was driving my car, still thinking about moving into the rash, when I mentally saw myself with two suitcases literally moving into this giant pimple. When I was inside, I looked around, noticing all the details and feeling the feelings that a rash might have. I thought the image stupid and released the vision. A few minutes later I arrived home rash-free!

A friend was later telling me about her rash. I told her of my experience, so she *"moved into her rash"* and hers disappeared, too. Yet another friend developed spots. When she asked why, her spirit friends responded:

> *To experience what others will in the future. You are repressing what you have chosen to do, and it is creating the lesions on your skin. It is around the earthly chakras because you need to address your earthly choices. When you have done so, and others come to you for guidance, you can "spot" their problems and identify with them. They will need this from you. You are not experiencing pain or discomfort, as it is not necessary for you, but others may. Be open to their pain--work to ease it for them when asked.*

## Strange Feelings----------

Strange, unsettling feelings almost always preceded a step-up in acceleration. They weren't exactly foreboding, but the sensations were always heavy and serious. I learned to recognize these as signals of something important that couldn't be ignored. A few of the spirit explanations follow...

*You are being adjusted. There are many layers from here to there. Each step must be carried out. Some you know about, some you do not. But all is in Divine right order. When you surrender to the highest good, you give permission to perfect your physical as well as your mental being. The physical imperfections must be purified in order to allow the physical to resonate and hold the higher vibrations. You are handling it well.*

*Just trust your inner knowing to give you direction. Rest, take it easy and you will be better than ever before long. This is an adjustment phase. Your essence of self, the highest self, is preparing to take permanent residence in your physical, but this cannot happen until the adjustments are made. Can you not tell?*

*********************

*Yes, dear one, you are again experiencing the restlessness that signals a new step. Your life is moving quickly. So feel the freedom and try not to hold on for security. It is the holding on that causes the difficulty. You must feel the security from within and release all else.*

*********************

*Your new feelings are the soul's stirring...beginning to get free. You see, now it is time to be you...YOU. You have taken off the layers of ego. Now you can begin.*

*You shall vacillate between the little you and big you for awhile, but soon you shall only be the greater you. Then you shall become the even greater you. Let beauty prevail.*

********************

*You are walking away from the old. It is gone forever. The familiar, the comfortable, are now in your past. There is a sadness, for you are leaving behind a part of you, the old you. You are entering this week a cocoon of sorts; when you return you will come back as a beautiful butterfly. Yes, the caterpillar does know it is leaving behind the old, slower, less effective form. But this does not mean that he leaves it without trepidation. For even though it was slow, it was him...who he was. So he enters this period of rebirth with the same feeling you are experiencing. Do not concern yourself with these feelings, my friend; they are part of your species. Keep your eyes on the light, feel the love, expect the beauty. You shall return as few on your planet have, as a butterfly of sorts. You shall feel the joy and your heart will sing. All is in Divine order. Trust. Walk in beauty.*

********************

*Yes, dear one, you are beginning to look back and reflect on your growth, and it is important that you do so. You have made a long journey. Now you must map the route so others may follow. Remember, you are a way-shower. Therefore you must always take the time to record and tell others before you go on. The journey is not complete yet, so you only take time to reflect, not discontinue. Many are close at your heels and wish you to hurry. Trust your guidance. The way is as important as the destination. Fill the path with love.*

Always the sensations were signals that announced progress was at hand. As you can see, there is no one-size-fits-all when it comes to physical adjustments. They are unique to the individual. Sometimes they make sense and sometimes they are weird, even to me. The best suggestion I can offer is to stay tuned in to your inner guidance and listen to its help. I have been given much wonderful information about the many transitions I have gone through, yet, it seems I continue to traverse the uncharted waters.

## *Personal Appearance----------*

I am not a vain person. I have never spent long hours in front of a mirror. I bathed and wore basic make-up which could be totally applied in a matter of a few minutes. I never retouched my make-up throughout the day. As my hair turned gray, I dyed it a respectable brown. (Although I did have red for a while) I had my hair permed at regular intervals but rarely saw a beautician between perms. Upon arising in the morning I would comb my hair and it would last the day. And that was the extent of my personal grooming. Yet my most challenging life lesson has been in this area.

First, I have very poor vision, which has always been corrected by contact lenses. I was married for seven years before my husband saw me in glasses, so that should give you an idea of how I felt about wearing glasses in public. Yet, as my frequency evolved I was no longer in harmony with contacts. I still don't know if it was the plastic or the fact that they smothered my eyes, but contact wearing came to a screeching halt. I was in mortal pain. I can move into a rash but don't expect me to be thrilled that I have to wear glasses in public. They are heavy and thick. They slide down my nose and require constant adjusting. I have astigmatism and have only a specific place to look through my glasses in order to see clearly...which is never where my eyes are looking.

I was mortified. How could my spirit friends allow this to happen to me. I had always been obedient to all I had been asked to do but this was too much. They had gone too far. This time I would not obey. This time I would resist.

I defiantly made an appointment with yet another eye doctor. Perhaps he would have the magic answer to my dilemma. I knew nothing could stop my quest for a new pair of tolerable contacts. After all, I had free will...My drive to the doctors office was to change that.

My first awareness that something was amiss was an uncomfortable sensation of wetness that seem to penetrate through all my layers of clothes. Yes, without any warning my bowels had discharged their contents. No warning was given. No time to prepare. My body had spoken loud and clear, and I was not to have contacts again. I did not then, nor now, like the decision but I have accepted it. I no longer resist the lessons that glasses afford me. The pain is beginning to subside. I still refuse to have pictures taken with my glasses. Maybe in time. . .

About this same time, I also found I could no longer tolerate any chemicals on my hair. My body would react with terrible flu-like symptoms. I could live without the perms, but giving up hair coloring was another great challenge. I didn't realize how gray my hair had become until it started to grow out. I had this terrible outgrowth that was practically white. I don't know how I looked but I felt terrible. I decided to get my hair cut short thinking that would make me look better. It didn't. Instead I looked like my seventh grade physical education teacher with gray roots. Everyone was polite but I wanted to bury my head until my hair grew back to its natural color.

I had a wonderful (or so I thought) idea. I would wear a wig until my hair grew out. I visited my friendly wig person and bought several. I bought different styles and colors. I didn't care if people knew I was wearing a wig; I did care when my gray roots showed. Wigs became hot and sweaty. They also shifted on my head during my busy lifestyle; remember I was the person who never checked the mirror. Several times at the end of the day, I found my own hair sticking out in a most unsophisticated manner. Now what; wigs weren't working. I made a bargain with God, the angels and anyone else who worked for the light. If they would protect me so I could get one last chemical process, I would live happily-ever-after as a gray-haired person. They accepted the offer. Much more, I might add, than did the beautician that was asked to frost my hair gray. She was horrified. She said it would make me look ten years older. She argued and did all she could do to talk me out of it. In the end, I won out. The gray frosting at least blended my gray hair with the rest of my hair. I could again go out in public!

The final straw occurred when I could no longer tolerate any make-up. I would claw at my face when any was applied, no matter the brand.

I had apparently entered my natural period of life. I do extensive traveling and talk to audiences of all sizes, and I felt I needed my make-up. I begged and pleaded with the universe to reverse the process. This was too much for me to bear. I felt naked in the world. I became much more aware of other women's make-up. I even envied their painted faces.

When I stopped struggling against my cruel fate, I was told that again my job was to lead the way. I must be able to walk in the world with no mask to hide behind. I was told it was my job to stand bravely with no facade to show others that it was okay for them to release *their* mask.

Sounds like others may also be asked to release their protective masks (although I never felt that processing my hair and make-up was a mask). If this should happen to you, all I can say is chin up, you will survive. I am still not happy about the changes, but it has simplified my traveling and shortened the time it takes to get dressed in the morning. I guess everything has a bright side if you are willing to look for it. Remember Viktor Frankl's famous words in his book, *Man's Search for Meaning,* "If it doesn't kill you, it will make you stronger."

## *Assorted Messages from My Spirit Friends*

lways when I needed them, my spirit friends were there for me. They guided me through the rough spots and cheered as I moved beyond them. The following messages of hope, inspiration, encouragement and guidance were given during various phases of my growth process. May they help you as they helped me.

*The way will be disclosed at every step. This does not override free will. We merely show the path. You must take the steps. Through love, trust and surrender to a higher purpose you indicate a desire for the path. We, too, do not desire to work when there is not the desire for cooperation. It is like a giant spiral. You indicate the willingness; we illuminate the way. You take the steps; we assist you over any real or perceived obstacles. You become stronger in your desire to follow the Radiant One. We make the way, the purpose and the plan more clear. It's as easy as that. For if we disclosed the entire project, mere mortals would run with fear. They would see themselves as unworthy.*

*Dear ones, you have held yourselves back so long with these thoughts. You call them humility, but truly they are not. Humility is simply the awareness of everyone's greatness, with no need to demonstrate your greatness over another.*

Doors were often used to illustrate the dimensional levels. These are the messages I received concerning the doors:

*There are six doors. You have opened the large one that leads to the awareness of the others. Desire opened that door. Many never make it through this door, nor even realize it exists. The next door shall not be so dramatic, but you shall be aware of them as you open them. They shall be doors of service and preparation. With each one a greater awareness shall be awakened. For truly you have progressed through all before. These too shall not be rushed but quietly and peacefully approached.*

Later, I was told...

*Just as doors open in your world to let you through or stay closed to keep you out, so, too, do the various dimensions. You have walked through four doors. You were told there were six. You are proceeding through the oft scary maze. The first door led you through into this new world. **Faith** opened that door. The second door brought many confusing and difficult tasks--**belief and trust** took you through that one. **Love** opened the third door. You had to love all unconditionally. Now you stand ready to walk through the fourth door. **Service** has been your key, for what good are your other qualities if service is missing? You willingly and unselfishly serve others. This has been your passport and it has been stamped "Succeed." You must find the* *keys for the other doors yourself. They will present themselves--you will recognize them. You must pick them up and proceed. Godspeed in the process. As you move through the sixth door you will find the kingdom of heaven here on Earth, and you shall help to anchor it to the beloved Earth. You are doing your part--and we, my friend, are doing ours.*

Amazingly, door four seems to be the most difficult for people to pass through. Apparently, by the time they get to door four, they have developed many special talents. It is at this point that many people put out a shingle and start charging fees. Unselfish service requires that you give of yourself without charge. Be aware so you do not fall into this trap. Have you noticed how expensive the spiritual path has become?

It is not always easy to give up old realities. The breaking up of old thought forms (which have a reality) can cause the feeling of spaciness and disorientation. This feeling is similar to the feeling of vertigo, only it is not in the physical; it is in your consciousness.

I heard a lot about the higher self before I really understood what it was. Finally an entity identified herself to me as my higher self. This is how she explained the process:

*I am the part of who you were when you decided the separation was needed. I became the anchor that kept you from going too far afield. I am the one who maintained the connectedness to the Creator's love. I have been your main support during your bumpy times. But as you recognize me and the role I play in your game of life, you are able to allow my consciousness to meld with yours; therefore, the separation no longer serves any point. As you stand in your own power and the Earthean illusions have no hold on you, then the need for the anchor is removed. You have your course chartered, so to speak, and nothing will blow you off course. I can now best serve you by again combining forces to work in unity with All-That-Is while in the physical. No longer do you need a connection outside yourself because you ARE connected and you know it. You will be all that you are, and you will be it while in the physical. Our combined energy and wisdom will assist Mother Earth and those in residence with what is to come.*

There was always a process of combining and accelerating energies. Always there was love.

*Yes, dear, we are here. It is good that you remind yourself of the love. For surely one can never over learn the lessons of love.*

*Your energy is being constantly adjusted. Soon we shall be as one. Your energy will be just as soft and gentle as mine. You are learning to control the Force now, only you feel it is the Force that is learning to control you. But it is not. You never give up control to another or to anything outside self. It is your inner wisdom that is learning to use, regulate and handle this extreme power. You had to surrender your ego self to your higher self before the Force was allowed to flow through you, for this much power in the wrong hands could cause untold damage. You are doing well. Your growth is steady and your confidence builds. Love is growing in your heart.*

\*\*\*\*\*\*\*\*\*\*\*\*\*\*\*\*\*\*\*\*

*Yes, dear child, all is well. You are still proceeding through much energy transfusion. For you see, time is short. You do not yet fully comprehend where you will be when this phase is complete. Energy is being given almost constantly and consistently. You are allowing it well. With this energy comes an opening to All-That-Is.*

\*\*\*\*\*\*\*\*\*\*\*\*\*\*\*\*\*\*\*\*

*Yes, love is growing in your heart and in your beingness. Have you noticed how seldom you lose your center? This is because you are raising your vibration, and the highest rate is pure love. . .unconditional love. Your students can do it for a brief second, but to maintain that vibration day in and day out while in physical requires a mental, physical and spiritual alignment to the Force. You are doing so more each day. Love is being in vibrational harmony with the universe...an energy of harmony where you are as one with all, including the Divine Essence. You are approaching that state of purity where any but the highest vibration would be quickly transformed and would resonate in harmony with you. Do you not see the changes in those around you? When the perfected vibration is permanent, then you shall learn to use the power of this frequency.*

*Those are the miracles that those in physicality speak of. But truly they are the feats that humanity was destined to perform. These were the behaviors that the Christ demonstrated to humanity; but instead of watching and learning, humanity instead fell to the feet of the great Master and tried not the lessons. On the other hand, if a quite ordinary person (like you) develop her skills, people will watch and model. They shall respect you, but not fall at your feet. It is the reason you have chosen ordinary features and ordinary brains and abilities. And when you say, "These things that I do so shall you do," people will listen, and most importantly, they will do. For you can take ordinary words and apply them to amazing feats and people accept. You can transform the wondrous to the acceptable. You shall ever be and are a great teacher. You do have the gift of simplicity. This shall serve you well.*

I debated whether or not to include this last message. As you can see, I decided to include it. It represents the reality that all of us *"ordinary"* people are destined for greatness. There is *Perfect Power in Consciousness.* If only you accept it, then all things are possible. This perfect power is not in competition or dominance, but is found in peace and harmony. The perfect power is the frequency you are when it is raised to that of the God source. Then you no longer take action; rather, you radiate, and all of the lesser frequencies are then altered to resonate to your frequency. You become the tuning fork that affects the world in a very positive way. I may be going along my path a little ahead of others, but the others must accept in their realities that all I do they too can do.

*You are still in transition. Do you not know and understand? The energies are still mixing. This is the reason for the rush, the extremes. These feelings will pass.*

It was often challenging to move into my new realities and have to deal with other people's reactions to them. As an example, my mother was very *concerned* for my well-being. She was sure that things were terribly wrong and was constantly trying to fix me. I was told to use humor...it worked.

*Humor is the oil of human emotions. Emotions have been described as the result of your reality bumping into the reality of another. Humor is a way of looking at those emotions in a lighter way. It allows us to learn from the experience and facilitates growth, where pure emotions can often hamper growth. Even love, as currently understood on Earth, causes us to get sidetracked. Humor, on the other hand, helps us look at them then move on. We are able to look at the emotion, release tension or stress, then move on with a pleasant detachment.*

There are four levels of knowing. The first level is called **unconscious incompetence**. At this level you don't even know that you don't know. An example would be the third-dimensional reality.

If you are in that reality, it is all you know; therefore, you don't even know you are stuck there.

The second level of knowing is *conscious incompetence*. At this point you recognize that you don't know. Although you still don't know, you recognize that you don't know. If you are in a third-dimensional reality yet recognize that other realities exist, you have actually grown even though at that point you may think it is hopeless because of the vastness before you. You may even feel more incompetent because you know you don't know. Recognize that when you begin to think you are stupid, it's actually a sign of growth.

The third level is *conscious competence*. At this level you have taken steps necessary to do it, or learn it, but it is still not a real part of you. It is still conscious work; it is an effort to change old behaviors or old beliefs and thought patterns.

The fourth and highest level of knowing is called *unconscious competence*. When you reach this point you're not having to think about anything because your habits are so ingrained that they are automatic. You radiate love without thinking about it; you allow each person his/her reality; you have given up all need for judgments, et cetera. You no longer have to think about this new behavior or knowing; it is part of you.

These four levels of knowing can be applied to any area in your life--learning to ride a bicycle, drive a car, jump rope or achieve any competence. My spirit friends told me...

*You are making progress. You have moved into what you lovingly refer to as conscious incompetence. Congratulations! One should never feel the lessons will end. For what would existence be without a purpose? It is the Divine will. You are at least recognizing it. You are realizing where you still hold on; you must now release and let God. You will find such a bliss as you do this! You do trust the Force, but old habits die hard.*

*Writing is a place where you "try"; but when you try, it comes from the ego/physical self--such a shallow place compared to All-That-Is. You asked for assistance and it is given. You recognize it, then you hold on...and hold on. You block your own progress. You are a little uncomfortable with the greatness or potential of such. This is natural, but do not block the thought of it. You must allow the thoughts. Plan for them; live them; make them happen. You are making satisfactory progress. You have planned for a slow start, so do not become concerned. All is in Divine order.*

As I open more to the higher frequencies and feel the joy they bring, I wonder why humanity ever lowered their frequencies to cause the breaking away. One day I asked, "Tell me of love. How did we first go wrong?"

*You on Terra have not gone wrong, for all paths of free will are filled with experiences and lessons. After all, free will allows you to examine life in the absence of love or love in a greatly diminished capacity. In the beginning there was God. God is Love. So in the beginning there was a perfect love. Love is all there is and was, but as humans wanted to explore all, they moved into various vibrations. As they did this, it caused the love/God/perfect vibration to be lowered. Never permanently. Because many, when they operate in physical/conditional love, can temporarily raise their vibrations to glimpse what was once a perfect condition. But one must remain in the perfected state of unconditional/unemotional love to stay in harmony with the God presence in all.*

During this process I was very drawn to crystals. I even went digging with a friend of mine. Since many people seem to be attracted to them, I offer this message:

*The crystals do serve you in many ways. First, they are receivers. They bring in many messages and energies, and help to attune you even further. Second, they assist to awaken you to the greater mission. They bring all that you need to know. We could tell you these facts but, as you are aware, this information would not be as real as that which you self-discover. This self-discovery helps to cement it to your life. Finally, you are learning to transcribe the message contained in the crystals. This, as you know, is a very important skill in the days to come. You are in the readiness phase; soon you will be crystal literate.*

I could fill volumes with messages which I have received, but that would serve no purpose. I would rather have you spend the time listening to your own inner guidance. Remember it speaks in a gentle soft and very small voice. Everyone has one but not everyone has the desire to hear it. I cannot imagine what my life would be like without it.

# *In Closing*

ll things must come to an end, and so it is with this book. I trust that it has made you think (the mind enjoys that), has added some new feelings to your physical sensations (your physical body enjoys that) and, lastly, has reminded you that your soul/spirit knows the way. All you must do is allow the process by releasing and letting go, thus empowering the wondrous soul/spirit.

A few years ago I taught a series of Sunday night classes on spiritual awakening and had a wonderful time. When the series came to an end, my spirit friends gave me a message to share with the participants. It seems appropriate to share it with you now. You, too, must continue without me. You, too, must find inner focus and learn to step out in faith. I am pleased that I could join you on your path, if only briefly.

*Truly they have learned much; but now the time comes for each to step out in faith. They must take action. They must trust. For, you see, in the search one can avoid responsibility and action. One can avoid the issue by looking around it. Whenever the search takes one away from the inner focus, it is mere activity, not growth. Each knows that, but they too fear the unknown as many do on Earth. When the time comes, they will develop trust. . .rather, when they develop trust, their time will come. For without trust their love and power will go unused, worthless in a time when there is such need. But free will must reign. Each must choose; each must have faith to step out into the service of the Radiant One--faith to look into the eye of self; to recognize and accept one's true self. Only then can one be called into active duty for the good of the universe and serve beside the great ones of all times. So turn your back on fear and darkness and move into the light, the love, the glory, the truth...the light!*

*As one marches on into the light, a transformation, rarely felt by humanity, will be complete and Terra shall come into full glory--the likes that dreams are made of.*

*Go in peace, love and the glory of the Radiant One.*

*Adonai*

# *Easy Steps to*
# *Perfect Power in Consciousness*

## To raise your frequency:

1.  Laugh--it's one of the quickest ways to accelerate your frequency.
2.  Cry--it cleans out old garbage and releases old emotions.
3.  Play--it requires you to enjoy, laugh and release control.
4.  Pray--this empowers the Divine Force in your life.
5.  Listen--3 minutes a day of quiet time in your place of center.
6.  Allow unconditional love in your life.
7.  Eliminate things that lower your frequency.
8.  Recognize there are many realities, and don't get stuck in one and don't feel the need to defend yours.
9.  Provide unselfish service *when asked.*
10. Sing--different songs do different things, so experiment.
11. Ask for help--there are many angels who are waiting to offer their hand in assistance.

## To purify your body:

1.  Get to know your body.
2.  Acknowledge your body is a good friend, but it is not you. *You are not your body*.
3.  Let your body make decisions about what it wants to eat and do.
4.  Allow your body to make adjustments without interference.
5.  Be nice to your body. Show your appreciation for all that your body does for you.

6.     Ask for help.

## To calm and control your mind:

1.     Recognize the mind's interference.
2.     Ask the mind to work in harmony.
3.     Calm the mind's fears.
4.     Take charge of your mind.
5.     Practice calming your mind and becoming receptive to Divine guidance 3 minutes each day.
6.     Allow the mind to evolve and be at peace with it.
7.     Recognize you have a mind, but you are not your mind.
8.     Honor your mind for all it does for you.
9.     Ask for help. The universe is willing to assist you.

## To allow soul/spirit to guide your life:

1.     Ask for guidance and protection.
2.     Give thanks to the Divine Force that guides your life.
3.     Develop inner focus. Learn to exist in the stillness and silence.
4.     Honor and follow your inner guidance.
5.     Allow unconditional love in your life.
6.     Trust that what you need you are given and what you are given you need.
7.     Trust in your own abilities and worthiness.
8.     Assist others upon request and always from your Divine Self.
9.     Ask for help.

**Dr. Heather Anne Harder**

501 S. Main Street

Crown Point, Indiana 46307

(219) 663-8282

Dear Reader/Friend,

This book has been a joy to write. I hope that my experiences and insights will help you recognize, allow and accept your own transformation with less trauma. If I can be of service, please feel free to contact me. I welcome your letters. I do love to hear your reactions to the material. If you would like to be on my mailing list, please send me your address. Several new projects are in process and will be released shortly. I will make "birth" announcements to all those on the mailing list at the appropriate time.

I would appreciate it if you would contact your local bookstores and mention this book and/or tell your friends about it. Do lend your copy if you are so inclined. It is information that needs to be disseminated. This personal and planetary transformation will occur. It will be most harmonious if humanity is prepared.

It is with peace, joy and light that I bid you goodnight and God's peace. I have enjoyed our time together.

Love and Light,

*Heather*

# *Bibliography*

Buzan, T. (1984). *Make the Most of Your Mind*. New York: Simon and Schuster.

Frankl, Viktor (1962), *Man's Search For Meaning: A Introduction to Logotherapy*. Boston: Beacon Press.

Guiley, R. E. (1991). *Harper's Encyclopedia of Mystical & Paranormal Experience*. California: Prelude Press.

Hampden-Turner, Charles (1981). *Maps of the Mind*. New York: MacMillan.

Harder, Heather Anne (1994). *Many Were Called, Few Were Chosen: The Story of the Earth-Based Volunteers*. Indiana: Light Publishing.

Harder, Heather Anne (1993). *Exploring Life's Last Frontier: The World of Death, Dying and Letting Go*. Massachusetts: Channel One Publishers.

Hill, Napoleon (1960). *Success Through a Positive Mental Attitude*. New York: Simon and Schuster.

Key, Wilson Bryant (1973). *Subliminal Seduction: Ad Media's Manipulation of a Not So Innocent America*. New Jersey: Prentice-Hall, Inc.

Keyes, Ken (No copyright). *The Hundredth Monkey*. Oregon: Vision Books.

Languis, M., T. Sander, and S. Tipps (1980). *Brain and Learning: Directions in Early Childhood Education*. Washington, D.C.: National Association for the Education of Young Children.

Lovelock, J. E. (1979). *Gaia: A New Look at Life on Earth*. England: Oxford University Press.

Lovelock, J. E. (1988). *The Ages of Gaia: A Biography of Our Living Earth*. New York: W. W. Norton.

Maltz, Maxwell (1960). *Psycho-Cybernetics*. New York: Simon & Schuster.

Ratcliff, J. D. (1975). *I am Joe's Body*. New York: Berkeley Books.

Restak, Richard (1979). *The Brain: The Last Frontier*. New York: Warner Communications.

Restak, Richard (1984). *The Brain*. New York: Bantam Books.

Roger, John and McWilliams, Peter (1991). *Life 101*. California: Prelude Press.

Russell, P. (1979). *The Brain Book*. New York: E. P. Dutton, Inc.

Watson, Lyall (1980). *Lifetides*. New York: Bantam Books.

**Dr. Heather Anne Harder** was a professor of Education at Governors State University in Illinois. She was awarded bachelor and master of science degrees in elementary education and a doctoral degree from Indiana State University.

Heather is the wife of Robert Alan and mother of two daughters, Kerri Anne and Stacie Elizabeth; these people have been her greatest physical source of joy.

Heather is also the author of *Many Were Called - Few Were Chosen: The Story of Earth-Based Volunteers* and *Exploring Life's Last Frontier: The World of Death Dying and Letting Go* as well as many articles which have appeared in local, national and international publications. Her writings range from effective parenting to past life experiences. She is comfortable in both scientific, fact-oriented and the *weird and wonderful* arenas.

Heather travels nationally and internationally to share the path of truth. This path leads through the fields of parenting, elementary and early childhood education. Some of the topics she shares with others are *Brain and Learning, Gender Fair Education, Stress-Free Education, Playing and Learning, Discipline and Classroom Management,* and *Nonverbal Communication.* Dr. Harder states, "Caring for and educating our children will determine our world of tomorrow. Their well-being is of vital importance if Earth is to ascend to a higher state of consciousness."

The path of truth also leads into a wide array of non-traditional subject matter. Heather has facilitated workshops on such topics as *Balancing Body, Mind and Spirit, Non-Verbal Communication, Spirit and Inter-Dimensional Communication, Death, Dying and Letting Go* and *Love: Awakening the Power Within.*

Heather began her journey to at-one-ment years ago. The path was neither direct nor well lit. Her inquisitive mind led her to seek truths from many sources. With guidance, trust and patience, she has learned much from her 'friends of the highest light.' Through her work, she now offers to show others a way to find their personal pathway to truth.

Dr. Heather Anne Harder has chosen to assist this country achieve its Perfect Power in Consciousness by seeking the Presidential nomination for 1996.

Governmental experience is teaching us that the ways of the past are not working in today's world. It is time for a loving transformation.

As a woman, her presence in the Oval Office alone will create a totally new atmosphere. The fact that she has never participated in the political field means she owes no one any "favors" and she cannot perpetuate a faulty system.

Dr. Harder, as a university professor, has shown her ability to ignite the spark of learning and fan its flames to produce a glowing light of knowledge. It has also served to teach her the value of guidance from those who are experts in their fields. That guidance will play an important part in her efforts to bring about the changes needed to recapture the true essence of a government for the people and by the people.

Dr. Harder has no illusions about the strenuous path she has undertaken, which is why she has begun her campaign early. Unlike those who work within the system, she has chosen to take her campaign directly to the people, just as she plans to do as President.

- If you are interested in having Dr. Harder speak in front of your organization to share her views and answer questions concerning her campaign for the office of President, contact either Deborah McGrew at (219) 662-7074 or Adrianne Bacavis at (219) 663-5011.
- While Dr. Harder is trimming away as much of the unneeded expense involved in campaigning for President, funds are still a necessary part of the process. If you feel so inclined any contribution may be sent to: The Committee to Elect Dr. Heather Anne Harder for President, 4104 Victoria Drive, Valparaiso, IN 46383 or call (219) 464-9744.
- For those wish to support Dr. Harder in the campaign process, there are a multitude of ways to assist. For further information contact Deborah McGrew at (219) 662-7074 or Adrianne Bacavis at (219) 663-5011.

# Introducing...

*The Association of Universal Light Volunteers (AULV)*

My spirit friend stated that it is now time for humanity to step forward and publicly claim their Light volunteer status. Therefore, the Association of Universal Light Volunteers (AULV) has been founded.

## The AULV Mission Statement and Affirmation

We, who gather in the glow of universal love, offer our services to all who seek them in whatever way we can assist and whenever called upon to do so.

## The AULV Purpose

1. To provide a forum to publicly acclaim one's intention of dedicating one's life energy for the well-being of Mother Earth, humanity, universal peace and harmony.

2. To provide a professional organization for light volunteers that endeavor on behalf of universal love and light.

3. To share growth experiences and offer light to others of like mind and purpose along the spiritual path of life.

4. To respect and honor the diversity represented on this planet and recognize the infinite wisdom which created diversity within all things.

5. To recognize and honor the oneness of all.

6. To promote a better understanding among all people and to find the common ground in all physical, mental, emotional and spiritual areas. No single ideology or "right" behavior is dictated by the organization. All who serve the Light walk a Divine Path.

7. To publish and disseminate (in a timely manner) universal truths as needed to bring about personal and universal harmony.

8. To provide a network to offer unselfish service for all those who seek to know truth and receive universal guidance at no cost.

9. To provide, at the least possible cost, opportunities for spiritual seekers to experience first hand the energies of sacred sites around the world.

## Corporate / Business Memberships

Corporate / business memberships are available for a $100 donation for those who wish to dedicate their business to serving the Light. With or without the donation, AULV's hope is that you make a public affirmation (silently or aloud) that you dedicate your business to bettering humanity and offering your business to serve the Light. When you affirm either silently or verbally, this empowers those of the highest Light to work through you and your business for the highest good of all.

All corporate and business memberships will be listed as sponsors on all AULV special events and conferences.

# AULV MEMBERSHIP FORM

_____

Name (Please Print)

_____

Address

_____

City                              State            Zip

_____

Daytime Phone                    Evening Phone

## MEMBERSHIP AGREEMENT

I am a light worker, a child of God, known by many names, who has come to Earth to bring peace and love to a troubled planet. In physical form I do not have to be perfect, I only have to do my best and do it with unconditional love. I have read and do acknowledge the organization's mission statement and will repeat it frequently in order to remind myself of my Divine purpose here on Earth.

I am enclosing my $5.00* membership fee. This covers the cost of processing my membership, my quarterly subscription to Light Reading, and my membership pin. These are to remind me of the Divine Light which I represent here on Earth.

_____

Signature                                      Date

_* You are welcome to decrease or increase your membership fee based on your financial situation. Membership money will be used to support the mission of the organization. All services are offered via unconditional love to all who indicate a need._

Return this membership application (or a photocopy) to:

## AULV
### 210 S. Main St., Suite 202
### Crown Point, IN 46307

For more information call the AULV office at: **(219) 662-7074.**

# BOOKS BY DR. HEATHER ANNE HARDER

**Many Were Called - Few Were Chosen: The Story of Earth Based Volunteers** is the story of Mother Earth, from her beginning to her current situation. It tells of her universal mission and the many volunteers who were sent to assist her when her well being was threatened. $10.95 soft cover.

**Perfect Power In Consciousness** describes the preparation needed to achieve inner harmony and spiritual ascension. It outlines the physical, spiritual and mental alterations that occur during this process both on a personal and a planetary level. The reader will discover that all experiences are opportunities to learn and grow in the school of life. $12.95 soft cover.

**Exploring Life's Last Frontier - The World of Death, Dying and Letting Go.** Leading Edge Review described this book by saying, "Heather Anne Harder, Ph.D., divides her inspiring new book into three sections. First she establishes her credibility; then she shares some of her experiences with the dimension beyond life; and lastly she discusses the process of transition into the next world and provides a technique to penetrate the limits of life while you are alive...A must for anyone exploring the limits of life." $15.95 soft cover

These books can be purchased from your local bookstore or you may order them directly from Light Publishing. Please add 15% for shipping and handling ($2.50 minimum). Send your check or money order to :

## Light Publishing
210 South Main Street, Suite 203
Crown Point, IN 46307

or call (219) 662-7248 for further information.